Only Believe!

#1300

A Spy Story, a Love Story and a Story of God's Great Miracles in Atheistic Russia

Hannu Haukka
with
Dan Wooding

WinePress Publishing Mukilteo, WA 98275

Foreword

"Only Believe" is a fascinating and challenging book that is truly a LOVE STORY.

It is the love story of Hannu Haukka for Laura, the girl that he so wanted to marry while she was trapped inside Communist Russia. How this drama played out will bring tears to your eyes.

However, the book is also a love story for the people of Russia and the other republics of what is now called the former Soviet Union by Hannu, who longed to bring them a message of hope after seventy years of atheistic indoctrination.

Hannu Haukka is a true visionary. He was used of God to get our CBN animated Bible series, "Superbook", translated into Russian and then shown on television in Russia during the dark days of communism. This was the first-ever showing of a Christian television program/ series in the USSR. This series based on the Scriptures brought an incredible response of more than a million letters from children in just four weeks.

I believe this breakthrough helped to pave the way for many other CBN programs that have now seen millions of people in the former USSR give their lives to Christ. This is a true end-times miracle.

Hannu, along with Laura have gone on to pioneer International Russian Radio/TV, and daily present the greatest love story ever to millions of viewers and listeners.

"Only Believe" is a powerful testimony of God's grace and what He can do with those who are totally submitted to His will. Once you have read it, you will not be the same.

Dr. Pat Robertson
Chairman
Christian Broadcasting Network

Contents

Chapter One

Russia, The Terrible

Icicles hung like stalactites from wet gutters of the carriage as I nervously drew back the cabin window curtain of the Helsinki-Leningrad train and peeked out into the snowstorm. Darkness had already fallen as the train screeched to a halt at Luzaika, the first stop inside Russia.

Snow, as thick as goose down, was tumbling helter skelter out of the gray, leaden sky, but still, through the murkiness, I could make out the figure of a Red Army soldier, his breath, with every exhale, puffing out white vapor into the below zero air. Snow was stacking up like a pyramid on his gray fur hat, and already covered a badge with the hammer-and-sickle on a globe with a red star above it signifying the authority of the Communist party, pinned on it.

The hand-picked frontier guard stood motionless, wrapped in a heavy gray trench coat, a thick brown leather belt also bearing an insignia of the hammer-and-sickle, girded his waist. Strapped on his back was a Kalashnikov automatic. Then I spotted other troops all dressed the same, and fluttering in the wind was the Soviet flag, a red field with a yellow hammer and sickle with a star above it.

1

What a welcoming party to what was called the "Iron Curtain" by Winston Churchill and later, the "Evil Empire" by Ronald Reagan. Thoughts of nuclear missiles, a never-ending Gulag that had swallowed up untold thousands of courageous Christians and other dissidents, the KGB, Lenin and Stalin, whirled about in my mind.

This trip came into being while I was studying at Bible School in Finland. It was there that I first heard about the plight of persecuted Christians in the Soviet Union. I learned that the 1917 Bolshevik revolution, led by Vladimir Ilyich Lenin, had set in motion forces that had caused cataclysmic changes in world history.

Christians, I was told, were deeply affected by the October Revolution as "dialectical materialism sought to rule out the supernatural." Religion was subjected to ridicule, oppression and rigid restriction. "Since the revolution, a generation of Russians have been told that '. . . both Moses and Jesus are mythical characters'" (The Unabridged Soviet Encyclopedia, Volume 5, p. 157)."

I was interested to see if this suppression had erased all remnants of religion so when a trip to Russia was announced, I immediately signed up. I had read somewhere that Alexander Solzhenitzyn, the courageous dissident, had said in the Gulag Archipelago, "I myself see Christianity today as the only living spiritual force capable of undertaking the spiritual healing of Russia."

I desperately wanted to be part of that healing. Of course we now know that the Church has survived and our party were to take in contraband Bibles for the underground believers who could not buy them for themselves. They were just not available in bookstores.

The year was 1971 and this was my first adventure behind the formidable barbed-wire border that stretched from the Baltic to the Black Sea. Being a Canadian citizen, I had never been confronted by an armed border guard before. The U.S./Canadian frontier between British Columbia and Washington state was, up until then, my only reference point. I had crossed the "Peace Arch" at the Washington State-British Columbia crossing many times and the officers had always given me a friendly smile and a "welcome" or "bon voyage."

As I continued staring through the train's window at the sullen Russian soldier, I silently asked myself, "Why would anyone want to carry a weapon like that at the border? There's nothing to shoot at." I was soon to discover that everyone from the West was considered by the Soviets to be an intelligence agent of a foreign government.

We had been well briefed by our guide, Raili Väisänen, who had traveled to the Soviet Union on many occasions. She had said that the Soviet border guards were infamous for their thoroughness in searching tourists.

It was like a scene from a spy movie - and the guards did come in from the cold.

Unwelcome perspiration beaded my forehead as the soldier boarded the train and began to examine our passports and then roughly rummage through our luggage with gauche manners. I silently echoed the prayer of Brother Andrew, the author of God's Smuggler who once said, "Lord, in my luggage I have Scripture that I want to take to Your children across this border. You made blind eyes see. Now, I pray, make seeing eyes blind. Do not let the guards see those things You do not want them to see."

The Lord did! I could hardly breathe as the man meticulously went through our belongings, but fortunately nothing untoward was found. After what seemed like an eternity, the soldier that was conducting the search left our carriage and moved on to check out other travelers.

"He really knows how to make us feel welcome," I whispered to one of my colleagues. He smiled and said nothing.

* * * * *

Our eventual destination was to be Petrozavodsk, the capital city of the Autonomous Soviet Republic of Karelia, located in the far northwest of Russia, close to the Arctic Circle on the shores of Lake Onega. The republic then had a population of about 1 million and portions of it had been seized by Finland during World War II and then recaptured by the Soviets by the end of the war. The trip from Helsinki would take some 36 hours of grueling travel. To get to this remote destination, tourists were forced to ride the night train first to Leningrad and then, after a day in this famous city, could that evening go on to Petrozavodsk. According to the train schedule, there were numerous departures from the showpiece city of Leningrad, created by Peter the Great as an "open window to Europe," but Western tourists were only permitted to travel during the hours of darkness, presumably to prevent them seeing the countryside, something I considered to be the ultimate in paranoia. There were reasons for this which included poverty and their military sensitivity. They were forty years behind the West and they didn't want to show that to the outsiders.

This meant a mandatory one-day stopover in Leningrad, the second largest city of the Soviet Union and its largest seaport. The fact that we were in the very place where Communism was first established in the world, added to the excitement of the trip for me. This was the city where the great struggle between atheism and Christianity had been birthed.

I was captivated with the beauty of Leningrad which some called the "Venice of Russia." Capitol of czarist Russia for more than 200 years, the city was a showcase of 18th century palaces and churches. Peter Tchaikovsky and Dimitri Shostakovich were two of the many famous composers who spent their lives in the city and studied at the Conservatory.

World War II brought extreme hardship to the people of Leningrad. From 1941 until 1943, the city was besieged by German soldiers. During that period, electric power and transportation were wiped out and water had to be carried from the river. Some 17,000 citizens were killed by bombs, while 640,000 more died of starvation.

The city lies on the Gulf of Finland in the delta of the Neva River. Spreading over mainland and more than 40 islands, it is cut by more than 80 river branches and canals, and linked by more than 300 bridges. Leningrad's ornate buildings and squares, erected by Peter the Great and his successors in the 18th century, have been carefully preserved. Just upriver was the Winter Palace, former residence of the czars and home of the world-famous Hermitage Museum.

But, we had not come to Leningrad to see the sights. Raili wanted us to utilize the time to visit the home of Paavo Lukas, a faithful believer in the local underground Baptist church.

Paavo lived in a small undeveloped suburb on the outskirts of Leningrad.

"Because it is located near a military training base," Raili solemnly warned us, "we need to be careful, as this area is out of bounds for tourists."

Our group took a bus to the sector where this man lived. We wore simple clothing so that we would not stand out from the ordinary Russian citizens — at least all except Timo, another Finn-Canadian who had been my friend for several years. This heavy-set 20-year-old decided to wear a bright pink shirt, blue jeans and collar-length hair. Our bus slowly waddled past the large-scale "paradise" housing developments where many of the people of Leningrad lived. We had passed by lines of glum people waiting outside of shops.

As we disembarked from the bus that had belched nauseating black exhaust smoke for the whole of the thirty-minute journey, Raili furtively checked around to make sure that we had not been detected. She then signaled us to follow her along a tired and beat-up street. We slipped and slid along in the slush as we walked to the home of Paavo.

Buried beneath our warm coats and, after one more glance up and down the street by our guide to make sure that we had not been followed, Raili rapped on the front door of a simple one-story home. After about a minute of nervous waiting, the door opened and there before us was the man who had suffered so much for his faith.

"Quickly," the short, stocky Russian said breathlessly, "please come inside."

We followed Raili into his humble abode and as the door slammed shut he hugged each one of us. "Thank you for coming," he said, tears of joy brimming in his dark blue eyes. "It is such a blessing to have fellow believers in my home."

"Sometimes we in Russia feel we have been forgotten by our brothers and sisters in the West, but when people like you come, it makes us realize that there are still those who care!"

Raili introduced each of us and we all sat down. Paavo's wife Aino, appeared in the simple parlor and he introduced us to her.

Thousands of miles from my home in Vancouver, I sat enthralled as I listened to the story of Paavo, the first Russian Christian I had ever met.

"I have probably had more run ins with the police in this area than anyone else," he began.

Paavo could see we thought this was because of his faith, so he immediately corrected this false impression.

"Initially," he said, "it was because of my drinking. Drunk as a skunk, I would often be pulled out of a ditch by the police. I was fabled for having an intimate knowledge of local ditches."

Paavo told us about his conversion to Jesus Christ and how the fact that he would hold "unregistered services" in his home brought down an even worse wrath from the police and the KGB.

Paavo explained that in Russia at that time, the Soviet authorities wanted churches to register with the Ministry of Religion and Cults. "They want to control what we do and preach," he stated firmly. "Our church group decided that we could not allow the atheistic authorities, a political system that mocked God, to tell us how to operate. This decision has caused us many problems, but it is a small price for us to pay to worship God in the way we want to.

"They consider me to be a counter-revolutionary and they have fined me many times for allowing my home to be used for these services."

Paavo then said, "Can you understand a society that fights something they don't believe in — God?"

We all laughed when he concluded with a quote from one of the police officers. "Paavo," he had said, "we are fed up with your unlawful activities. It would have been better if you had stayed in the ditches."

Time rushed by and night had fallen from the sky like a heavy blanket. It was now time to depart Paavo's home and head back into the big city to catch the night train. Before we left, Paavo warned us, "You need to be very careful as the military will be loading equipment at the local train station. You will pass by the loading zone to get to the bus. If they challenge you, don't answer. I'll be walking behind you, so wait and let me do the talking."

As we headed out into the street, we pulled our over-coats tightly around our shoulders. The heavy rains of the afternoon had turned the dirt road by his house into a combi-nation of slush and mud and night mist covered the sidewalk.

When we arrived by the railroad tracks, we noticed a con-siderable amount of military activity. Soldiers were busy load-ing armored personnel carriers and tanks onto a special mili-tary train. For me it was an unsettling sight. I had never seen a real tank before. Now, here were lines of mobile armor.

I was walking with Timo when a soldier stepped out in front of us and lifted his rifle and pointed the barrel straight at me. We both froze in our tracks as he began shouting at us to "halt."

Paavo, who was about a dozen yards behind us, raced to catch up with us.

"Please, sir," he pleaded in Russian, "don't shoot. These are friends. They mean no harm. They are just catching the bus back into the city."

After a brief exchange, the soldier lowered his weapon and waved us through. It turned out that we should have detoured around the loading zone instead of walking through it.

Russia was indeed turning out to be a terrible place to visit.

* * * * *

The night train arrived in Petrozavodsk at 7 o'clock in the morning. Raili had told us that Intourist guides would meet us at the train station. "They set the program for all tourists," she had explained. "That is why visits to private homes are difficult to arrange. In fact, contacts with local residents are strongly discouraged by these guides."

Even though the train was a good half mile long, our Intourist hosts knew exactly where to find us. They welcomed us and then asked us to get into a Volga to go to the govern-ment-run Northern Hotel. The city with a population of about 240,000 people looked melancholy, dull and gray. All the build-ings appeared to need a good coat of paint.

"I am arranging for us to leave the hotel and meet with a couple of faithful believers in the city," explained Raili over breakfast. "We will rendezvous in the lobby in ten minutes."

Our group quickly headed out into the streets. I noticed that nobody wanted to make eye contact with us. After a brisk walk in the sub-zero air, we were able to meet up with Vera and Laura, two local believers, on a street corner.

Laura took my eye. She wore her dark hair in a bun and had sparkling blue eyes. "Welcome to our city," she said warmly as she shook hands with each one of our party. I felt my heart skip a beat as she clasped my hand.

"Would you like to visit an underground church?" Laura asked brightly.

We all nodded. I had heard a lot about the persecution of believers in the Soviet Union. I was aware that many had been arrested, tortured and imprisoned. Now we were to meet with a whole group of them.

Something incredible was about to happen to me.

Chapter Two

The Hawk's Nest

My thoughts were jumbled up as I settled down for the long flight. My first trip into Russia had been extraordinary and I had enjoyed my time at the Bible school in the country of my birth, but now I was pleased to be returning to the familiarity of my adopted land and the sanctuary of the "Hawk's Nest" that my parents and brothers provided.

As the jet left behind a trail of blue exhaust in the night sky, I decided to pass the time on the flight by piecing together how my family had ended up in Canada.

My mind initially focused on 1957, the year we made the move from Finland. It was a year that had seen American singers like Bill Haley, Buddy Holly and Elvis Presley, pioneer a form of music called rock-and-roll that had taken the world by storm. Many Finns wanted to move to North America, not for the music, but to see if they could capture for themselves some of the wealth, excitement and freedom.

From 1939 to 1944, Finland had fought a terrible war with the Soviet Union and had miraculously retained its independence in contrast to Estonia, Latvia and Lithuania, which in

1945 fell under the yoke of Soviet oppression. Even though Finland, a relatively small nation of 5 million people that spoke its own peculiar language, had kept its freedom, the government had surrendered some of its territory to the Soviet Union in exchange for peace. Squeezed between monarchical Sweden to the west and the giant Soviet Union to the east, Finland had been under occupation by both — most recently the latter. Finland obtained independence from Czarist Russia in 1917, the year of the Bolshevik Revolution.

Many older Finns said that it was their "believing prayers" that saved the nation. I was told that all of Finland had been on its knees praying that God would intervene as the Red Army marched west, crushing Finnish defenses one by one. Finland was spared, but was forced to sign a friendship and cooperation agreement with her powerful eastern neighbor.

At the turn of the century, the first wave of massive emigration to the United States and Canada had begun. Now, during the years of 1955 - 1958, the second wave were again leaving the "mother country." Once more, multitudes of Finns were busy packing their few belongings and heading for North America in quest of a better life for themselves and their children. Undoubtedly, many were concerned by the possible military aggression from their eastern neighbor, who was still smarting from its failure to add Finland to its great empire.

The Finns had good reason to fear another invasion. In 1956, the Hungarian uprising had been mercilessly crushed by Russia with whom Finland shared one thousand miles of frontier. After flexing their muscles in Hungary, what could stop the Soviets from taking over Finland? It seemed that only time would tell.

One person who did not want to wait for that cataclysmic event to occur was Seppo Haukka (Haukka means hawk in English), the father of three boys, Markus, 4, Hannu, 3, and one-year-old Juha, along with his wife Anneli.

Dad had told Mum one day in 1957 the news. "Anneli," he said, his face visibly excited, "we are going to make a new life in Canada."

Although we didn't know much about Canada, it sounded good to us. My parents had decided that Canada offered more opportunity to us at that time in the fifties. Another factor was that the U.S.A. was not as open to Finns at that time.

So, with my father wearing his only suit and mother in a summer dress and us boys in one-piece overall-type vest/pants combinations, the "fearless five hawks" boarded an Air France four-propeller aircraft bound for the predominately French-speaking city of Montreal. The long flight was not without incident. During a violent thunderstorm, an engine suddenly caught fire and the whole aircraft listed violently to the left. People began to scream with fright. The captain was able to complete the rest of the journey with three engines. The fire in engine four had apparently burned itself out.

We all breathed a sigh of relief as we touched down safely at Montreal's international airport and were welcomed by an immigration official as "landed immigrants". We missed our connecting flight to Sudbury because neither mom nor dad knew any English and could not understand the call to board the flight. So a day later they flew to that northern Ontario town where the "Hawks" established their first nest.

We soon began to integrate into a society where many of the city's inhabitants were of French descent, though most could also speak English. We "Hawks" knew neither language. However, the acclimation process was cushioned by the care shown to us by the Finns already settled in the area.

Sudbury offered my father much better prospects of employment and also had a larger community of Finns than Montreal. Located about 250 miles north of Toronto, Sudbury was a peculiar city being one of the major nickel producing centers on the North American continent, and in the world. Its barren sulfur-burned hills looked more like a moonscape than a landscape. Not a green tree existed within miles of the pollution-spewing smoke stacks of the nickel mines. They belched black poison gas into the atmosphere around the clock. The nightly spectacle of flowing and glowing, red-hot lava-like slag dumped on slopes surrounding the mine was the number-one attraction for tourists — and lovers.

A small, 300-square foot wooden shack on Ontario Street owned by Mr. Mäki, an immigrant from Finland, became our home. Paint had long since peeled off the outer walls of the house. It consisted of a kitchen and one room which doubled both as a living room and a bedroom. The rent was $25 a month, which compared well with the going rate of $75 for similar properties in town. The place was nothing to write home about, but the front yard was large enough for three young ruffians to play in without being threatened by passing cars. The next year, in 1958, a fourth son, Jyrki, was born.

"Daddy Hawk" eventually found employment working in the logging camps. Finns had a reputation of being unbeatable laborers and unbeatable drinkers. Fortunately, as a Christian, my father was only in the first category.

The logging camps were located far enough to limit his visits home to twice a month. Still, the paychecks came in without fail. Soon, news from Elliot Lake, which was 80 miles west of Sudbury, reached the Finns that better pay could be had in the uranium mines of this remote northern Ontario town, so we made our next move there. We lived in Elliot Lake from 1958 to 1963 in a small, inexpensive three-story apartment to start with and later, a rented split-level brick house. It was the first taste of prosperous North American life for our family.

In the fifties, Elliot Lake was the undisputed uranium capital of the world, with most of its exports going to the United States. Its residents, predominately French Canadians, knew virtually nothing of the possible health hazards connected with living in an uranium mining town. At that period, nuclear waste and radiation was not a concern. Elliot "Lakers" treated it as if it were coal.

However, the local health authorities began to investigate the situation and, realizing the imminent danger to the local residents, closed down the mines and in the late sixties the town was almost completely evacuated. The population dropped sharply from about 50,000 to 6,000. Radioactive pollution was killing the fish in the surrounding lakes from which the town drew its drinking water. Although Elliot Lake is still open and some mining continues, the authorities still continue to warn sports fishermen and residents not to consume larger, older fish, caught in the surrounding lakes.

Among the residents of Elliot Lake were a handful of Finnish families. Before the evacuation began, we attended a local Pentecostal church. The building was under construction when we first went to the services. We would worship in the basement, with no visible structure above the ground. Later, a sanctuary and ground-level facility arose to decorate the barren lot owned by the church.

Although I was brought up in a Christian home, I had not yet had a conversion experience. I can still distinctly remember one beautiful sunny morning in March when I attended a Sunday School class and I heard, once again, about the love of Jesus Christ and how He wanted to come into my life and forgive me of all my sins. My class had a good teacher who told Bible stories in a spellbinding manner. Class was dismissed and the children were led into the main class where the adults were having their own study.

It was during that meeting that at the age of seven I closed my eyes and began to pray, "Lord God, I want to give my life to You. Please forgive me for my sins and come into my life." A sensation of extreme happiness flooded my body.

As I left the church that morning, I traipsed through the thick snow as the sun shone in a clear blue sky. I sang "Jesus Loves Me This I know," all the way home. I burst in through the kitchen door. "Mom," I exclaimed, my face ablaze with excitement, "I have given my heart to Jesus."

She hesitated for a brief moment to take in the full meaning of what I had just told her and then she flung her arms around me. With deep joy, she muttered, "Thank God! Oh, thank God!"

Hannu at age five with his older brother Mark.

A Haukka family picture in the uranium Capital of the world, Elliot Lake, Ontario. (L to R. Hannu, Mark, Anneli, John (Juha), Seppo and Jyrki)

Chapter Three

Go West, Young Man

My father ripped open the letter with unconcealed excitement. Postmarked "Los Angeles," he knew it was from his older brother, Pentti. Dad read out loud the handwritten letter. "You should move here," he said. "Los Angeles is a wonderful city where the sun shines every day of the year and there are plenty of well-paying jobs."

I could see from my father's flushed face that he had "taken" the bait. We had all endured enough of the bitter winters of northern Ontario and Dad was impressed that Pentti, despite his linguistic and other academic skills, could'nt get work which he qualified for, still had managed to pick up a good paying job as a carpenter in "The City of Angels."

Pentti had moved there from Sudbury with the assistance of a loan of $2,000 from my father, and so wanted partly to repay his brother's kindness with this suggestion to "Go west, young man."

So we packed up a trailer towed by my Dad's 1959 Pontiac Strato Chief, and on June of 1963, we began the long journey to the west coast of Canada and then down to Southern California. "We'll stop off in Vancouver before driving down the coast," my father announced as we started our marathon journey through the wide open prairies towards British Columbia. It took seven days of concentrated driving on the Trans-Canada Highway to make the 2,700 miles to Vancouver.

When we arrived, we were all captivated by the beauty of Vancouver. Its wide harbor which is crossed by the Lion's Gate and Second Narrow's Bridge was breathtaking and its 130 parks, including the 1,000 acres occupied by Stanley Park, gave the city an added splash of beauty. Crowning everything was a row of majestic mountains highlighted by Grouse Mountain, 3,974 feet high, which provided excellent ski slopes in the winter, and had a mountain top that could be reached by an aerial tramway. The city had a spirit and vibrancy that took us all by surprise.

We stayed temporarily with the Itkonens, a Finnish family of three teenage boys and one girl, in a house in the suburb of Richmond, making twelve of us living under one roof. To complicate matters, another large family arrived from eastern Canada, making a total of eighteen of us in that one house.

It was while we stayed there that Otto Itkonen introduced my father to salmon fishing. Soon Pa was standing on the deck of a Finnish troller as the boat ploughed through the azure waters of the great Pacific Ocean. He smiled as he sucked in large gulps of the bracing air into his lungs. He admired the rugged rocky coastline covered with a carpet of pine and cedar trees and the magnificent marine fiery red-ball sunsets, as well as the peace and the absence of city noise. Just one fishing trip was all he needed to make a decision. The family would stay in Canada.

Dad was soon able to find us a more permanent home on Venables Street close to the P.N.E. in Vancouver East and also purchase his own commercial fishing troller with the money he had made as a miner in Elliot Lake.

During the salmon fishing season, which lasted from April to October, he fished the waters off the west coast of Vancouver Island all the way up to Cape Cook, close to the northern tip of the Island. He would also take the troller down to the Washington State border. It wasn't all fun, for my father. When he would fish off Swiftsure Bank and Big Bank off Vancouver Island, he was aware that the waters could be treacherous for marine traffic. Also, vicious spring and fall storms and fog would spring up claiming the lives of sea men each year. My father was away from us for extended periods of time. Consequently, my mother assumed the responsibility of bringing up the children. During summer holidays from Argyle Secondary High School in North Vancouver, we boys would take turns in "deck-handing" on the boats, earning quick cash for ourselves.

It was while at sea that I got my first insight into Russian life. Huge freighter-size Soviet trollers, including floating canneries, regularly swept the limits of Canadian territorial waters looking for fish. At times, we would count over 50 vessels in a single Soviet fleet. I would stand by the ham radio and listen to Russian being spoken over it. To my ears, it sounded like a harsh language riddled with "zeds" and "esses." It was certainly not a tongue I ever wanted to speak.

* * * * *

As a young man in western Canada, the realization that God had a plan for my life came fairly early in my life.

My family had joined a local Finnish Pentecostal church and one morning there was a guest preacher from neighboring Naselle, across the border in Washington state. I am sure that Pastor Albert Wirkkala, a fellow Finn, had preached well that morning, but my hyper-active mind had found it difficult to focus on what he was saying.

I heaved a sigh of relief as the service ended with a closing prayer from the visiting preacher. Jumping out of my seat, I headed for the main entrance. My mother caught up with me and reached out her hand to catch me in mid flight. She held my hand tightly as she began talking to Albert and his wife. She wanted them to meet her sons and I was the first she was able to "capture." "My greatest prayer, dear friends, is that my boys become real followers of Jesus and eventually become missionaries," she told the pair. She did not know that I had a different agenda as a red-blooded youth before I got too deeply involved in serving God.

Albert, however, did not need any more encouragement. He stretched out his hand, laid it on my head and began praying loudly, "Lord, you see this young boy's life. Protect him and bless him. Use him in service for your Kingdom, as you wish. In Jesus' name. Amen."

By now my face had flushed to beet red. I glanced around hoping none of my peers had seen what had just occurred. Prayer had been the last thing on my mind at that moment. I had joined in prayer with my parents at home as we sat around the table, or at my bedside with my mother seated beside me, in Sunday School, but not after church on my way out as my friends could see me. I just wanted to be outside with them.

Yet, invisibly, inexplicably, Albert's prayer sank into the depths of my heart. It would return to me time after time in the years to come.

That prayer came to fruition some years later when I had reached the age of fifteen. A short, stocky American evangelist had come to Vancouver to conduct an evangelistic campaign. The 1,000-seat auditorium of John Oliver High School was packed full each night.

Rumor had it that miracles were taking place and the sick were being healed at these meetings. I had never seen a healing take place, so with great anticipation I attended midweek service with my family.

From my seat at the side of the middle section of the auditorium, I figured I could get a bird's eye view of everything that might take place. The first part of the service was dominated by corporate singing of worship songs. Then the diminutive figure of the preacher stepped out onto the stage and he began to preach. I hadn't seen any miracle healings take place, but something perhaps more extraordinary was about to occur.

Halfway through his sermon, the evangelist paused and let his eyes sweep the congregation. In his distinctive voice, he said, "I feel led by the Holy Spirit to stop preaching for a moment. I want to call some of the young people here up to the front."

His voice had a power as it rolled through the sound system set up at the rim of the stage. He paused for a moment to allow the words to sink in. "There are five young people here tonight and in your lives there is something special that God wants to do."

I felt a surge of electricity tinge the air. It was so powerful you could almost reach out and touch it. As I sat

18

there, transfixed, the evangelist began pointing out young people around the hall. One by one, they stepped forward. I was amused. I thought to myself, this is great witnessing God calling people like this. Then he pointed directly at me. "You," he said, his eyes now fixed on mine. "Yes, the one sitting at the end of the row." My heart began to thump wildly. I looked around, hoping desperately he didn't mean me, but no one else moved. By now, every eye was focused on me. I was sitting in my seat, leaning on the armrest with my hand on my cheek. "You, with your hand on your cheek, leaning on your armrest. I mean you. You come!"

In an involuntarily response, I stood up and began walking towards the front of the platform and joined the four young people already standing there. In a daze I looked up at the preacher. I had attended the service out of curiosity, but now I was suddenly part of the action. I stood shoulder to shoulder with the others who had come forward. "God has a special task for each of you," the preacher said with deep conviction in his voice. "He will use you. I want to pray for you and bring God's blessing on your life. You will need God's special protection, His blessing and grace, in order for His will come to pass."

Then the evangelist stretched out his hands in our direction. He was not close enough to touch us. What happened next is something I still cannot explain. My world tilted up at a skewed angle as I suddenly keeled over backwards. I can remember lying on the floor with tears streaming down my cheeks. I lay there for several minutes with tears of joy wetting my face. I could feel the wonderful ministering presence of the Holy Spirit. Looking back, I can only say that it was a concrete visitation of the Lord on my life. It was something that I had not felt ever before.

The other young people had apparently experienced the same supernatural encounter that I had. When I finally, rose to my feet, I was astonished at what had taken place yet I felt curiously strengthened and refreshed. I walked back to my seat, conscious that somehow I would never be the same again. Regarding my life, something had indeed happened in God's invisible world. As I eased myself down into my seat, I began to wonder how God could use someone like myself. Certainly

there was nothing special about me. My father was a fisherman and my mother was—a great mother. Our family was
not rich or famous. There were no brilliant or talented individuals in our family tree. Surely there had been some kind of
mistake.

I was to find out that God does not make mistakes!

Chapter Four

Laura

Snow was falling heavily on that day in January 1945, when a Russian train meandered along the tracks towards a destination that was unknown to the group of Finnish-speaking men, women and children, huddled together for warmth in a cattle boxcart in the sub-zero temperature. But the driver of the train, and the engineer who kept the engine well stocked up with coal, knew that they were heading to a remote village in central Russia.

The bloody Second World War was well over and the return of the Inkeri minority from Finnish soil had gone well for the Russian authorities.

For hundreds of years, this small offshoot of the Finnish people had lived on a patch of land the size of Maryland in and around St. Petersburg (later Leningrad) offering the Russians the fresh produce off the Inkeri farms they ran so efficiently. The war between Finland and Russia had been vicious, producing some 50,000 casualties on the Finnish side and 200,000 on the Russian.

As the war front advanced, the inhabitants of the Inkeri village of Krásnoye Selo had scattered in the face of the advancing Nazi Army. The Heimonen family fell hostage and was hauled off to a Nazi detention camp, not far from Leningrad. Conditions behind the barbed wire were primitive. Death was an everyday occurrence. Epidemics raged a war and mercilessly reaped a terrible toll of the innocent. Sickness was no respecter of persons and the Heimonen's two daughters, Salme, aged four and Mary, five, both died from diphtheria. Medication was not available as young and old fell victim to the illness.

Eventually in 1941, the gates to the detention center had swung open. During their time of incarnation, the camp had fallen under the control of the advancing Germans from the south. After releasing the prisoners, the Nazis commanded the refugees to head west towards Estonia. Consequently, John and Eva had launched out on their 300-mile trek by foot with their remaining daughter, Inkeri, bearing the same name as the tribe they came from. They all wore Russian fur hats and tried to shield themselves against the punishing winter temperatures by wearing padded clothing and felt boots.

A grieving mother's sorrow is unfathomable. Only those who have experienced the loss of a child, let alone two, can understand it. Eva could have just as well as headed for the cemetery where her two daughters were recently buried. Her will to live had evaporated with the passing away of the children. John, a man in his mid-thirties with straggly brown hair and dark, blue eyes, had scraped up enough money to hire a Russian "burden bearer" to carry Eva's remaining daughter, Inkeri.

One night on that terrible journey, John and Eva slept under a bush. As Eva was sleeping, she began to dream that a young man dressed in pure white had approached her. "Please give me Salme and Mary," urged the stranger, as she saw herself holding on tightly to her two daughters. Eva did not want to part with them. The stranger spoke again. "You cannot take them where you are going," he said gently. "Just give them up to me and all will be well." After some resistance, Eva surrendered them to the stranger and then watched the man in her dream take her two girls down an uneven potholed road as he held their hands. They made their way to the bank of a river. He then proceeded to take the children, one by one, over a stream. From there, they continued towards the summit of a mountain.

In her dream, Eva stood on the other side of the stream and admired a beautiful field of flowers. Suddenly, she heard Mary cry, "Mommy," and then hold up a beautiful bouquet of flowers. Eva shouted out, "Pick longer ones." At that point, Eva woke up. Her sorrow had come to an end. She understood that a messenger from heaven, an angel, had taken her children to a better place.

* * * * *

The war was over but the Inkeri people found no peace. Under German occupation, Estonia had welcomed them. Then came the Russians. After about three years, all those with Finnish surnames were to be expelled from Estonia. The Heimonen family, were again detained in a prison camp. This one was called Ostrova.

Another winter was spent behind barbed wire.

They were eventually released by the Germans who were busy with the siege of Leningrad. But all was not well with this siege. Members of the Inkeri tribe intuitively sensed that it would be wise to flee to neighboring Finland. But they were not even safe in Finland, for when the war finally ended, a peace agreement was signed between Finland and Russia, in which all Soviet residents would be forcibly returned to the USSR and were deported to an unknown destination.

As dawn broke and the snow continued to float down from heaven, the train came to a grinding halt at the Krestsy station. The train soon emptied of its passengers. Krestsy was apparently a random choice for the authorities. There was no logic in the decision except to splinter the Inkeri people and spread them throughout Russia, thus prohibiting uncontrolled contact among them.

Along with others, the Heimonen family clambered out onto the ground. John helped his wife, Eva, onto the platform and they then both held out a hand to guide Inkeri onto the platform. Eva was eight months pregnant and felt the new life jump within her as if that new child was also scared about what lay ahead.

A uniformed militia officer was there to "welcome" the various Inkeri families to their new hometown. "You will be responsible for finding places to live," he said as his breath vaporized in the cold. "We have got you this far, now it's up to you." With that, he turned and walked away into the train station office where a cheery coal fire greeted him.

The pale morning sunshine glistened in the snow. Eva and her daughter waited at the station while John went on his scouting mission. He soon found a tenderhearted elderly Russian woman by the name of Marie who graciously had mercy on the family and opened her home to these unexpected refugees.

Shortly after they had moved into Marie's humble wooden home, Eva's birth pains began. John managed to walk his wife to a nearby hospital and soon Laura Anneli was born. The date was February 20, 1945.

After several years in Krestsy and the surrounding area shoveling peat and doing carpentry, John decided that he would move the family north to Karelia, so he could take work there as a logger in the pine forests. They traveled by train to their new home. The locomotive came to a complete stop as it pulled up alongside the station platform in Petrozavovdsk, a city of 300,000, situated about 250 miles northeast of Leningrad (St. Petersburg) above the 60th parallel. The city was founded in 1703 by Peter The First, and the name literally means, "Peter's Factories."

The family had again traveled in a humble boxcar and little Laura had woken up to the splattering of cow pie. It was May Day, the high, holy day of communism in Russia. A day when the trinity of Marx, Engels and Lenin, were worshiped as part of the religion of communism. The Communist party of the Soviet Union had cynically decided to tap into the religious inheritance of Russia by creating its own religion. They had holy days and even their own hymns—in praise of the great October Revolution. Later that day, not only Red Square in Moscow, but squares in all major cities throughout the Soviet Union, would be full of worshipers.

An Inkeri friend met the family at the Petrozavodsk station. He quickly offered John some good advice. "You don't have to go logging here," he said. "You can stay in the city and do construction work instead." John didn't need any further exhortation. A government construction company offered John and the family a single room in a bug-infested former German prisoner of war barracks. The place consisted of one-story log houses with about 16 rooms, eight on each side of a center aisle. Nineteen families were jammed into the compound.

"I'm afraid that you will have to share your room with another family," John was told by the camp commandant. This meant that nine people were forced to live in one room together. For ten long years, the Kukonmäki barracks served as home for the Heimonen family. Young men from the Inkeri minority frequently clashed with their Russian counterparts who were also domiciled in the area. There were fist fights and other clashes of a racial nature that included weapons such as leather military belts and knives. The Russians nicknamed the street adjacent to the barracks as "Helsinki."

However, not all was bad inside the barracks. A group of "free evangelicals" regularly conducted evangelistic Finnish-language meetings there in a nearby hall. Those passing by could hear the gusto singing of hymns like "What a Friend We Have in Jesus." Both her mother, Eva, and cousin, Vera, had made decisions to follow Jesus Christ as a result of the meetings. But, even though Laura enjoyed the singing and preaching, she still was not ready to make that life-changing decision. Her father John, did not like the services at all and would usually stay in his room drinking vodka. His wife's faith often provoked him to angry responses, usually when he was drunk. "I don't believe in all this God stuff," he would shout. "John, please don't yell like that," she would say, holding up a placating palm. "God loves you and wants to help you with your drinking problem." This would provoke him to even more violent behavior. "What problem?" he would yell. "I don't have a problem. You are the one with the problem. You are believing in someone who doesn't exist."

On one occasion, Aino, a frail, small-statured, dark-haired ethnic Finnish believer who also lived in the barracks, hurried into the Heimonen family home. She had stumbled across a Christian broadcast on short-wave radio.

By 1959, the Soviet Union boasted that there were over 100 million short-wave radio sets in the country, but there was also a network of 2,500 jamming stations set up to try and block out the signals that were pouring through the Iron Curtain from around the world. Somehow, this program had evaded the awesome Communist network of jammers.

Aino felt she had uncovered gold when she first heard the "Good News" in programming provided by a group of Finnish Pentecostals through IBRA (International Broadcasting Association) based in Finland. These dedicated broadcasters had begun broadcasting from North Africa due to the lack of access to government radio facilities in their homeland. Because of geo-political considerations, no type of Russian language programming was permitted from Finnish soil. Little did the producers of this program, which was in Finnish, realize what impact their efforts would have in the sizable community of the so-called "lost" Finns.

"You must listen to this program," Aino said breathlessly. "It is in Finnish and there is a man telling about God's love. It comes from Radio Tangier. It is very wonderful to listen to." This elderly bilingual widow loved tuning into her radio, but most of the Christian broadcasts were in the Russian language which she and most of the other Finnish-speaking Christians could not understand. These short-wave broadcasts had become the lifeline to the persecuted church of Russia.

John was out at the time, so Eva switched on the large brown radio and began twiddling with the knob until the signal came in loud and clear. It was now late at night, but none in the family was sleepy as they listened in awe to the voice of a preacher explaining God's wonderful plan of salvation.

Little Laura was particularly impacted by the message she heard that night coming out of the sky from many miles away.

Father Ivan, Inkeri, Laura and mother Eva during the height
of Russian Communism.

Chapter Five

Ideological Warfare

Laura had begun to blossom from an awkward pre-teen into a beautiful sixteen-year-old young woman. Besides turning the eye and a plethora of admirers who came into her life, other new things also began to happen to her. Firstly, the family, after ten long years in the barracks, were able to move into a wooden two-story construction. This primitive, no frills, condominium had two rooms covered with rose-pattern wallpaper, but no hot water, no heating other than a wood stove-furnace in the living room. Secondly, she decided to continue her studies at the four-story University of Petrozavodsk located in the city center. Laura's greatest ambition was to become an eye surgeon.

As she walked the huge campus, whose most famous student was Yuri Andropov, the one-time head of the KGB and later the Soviet Communist Party Chairman, right after Leonid Breznev, she became aware that the new bold climate of "intellectual atheism" that permeated this institute of higher learning had begun to rub off on her, causing the spiritual influences of her childhood to vaporize into thin air. The faith of her mother no longer remained an influential force in her life as she became engulfed in her studies of dialectic materialism, physics, chemistry, literature, anatomy, Latin, English, physiology, political history and economics. Friends, too, seemed to multiply as she drew quality marks in all subjects. There was now no time for God or religion.

Laura's family had divided into two distinctive ideological camps. On one side was mother Eva, sister Inkeri, who had also become a Christian, and cousin, Vera. They had all found a living faith in God. On the other was her father, John, who proudly declared himself to be an atheist. Laura found herself at that time to be in the same camp as her father.

Life on the campus went smoothly for Laura until the third semester. Every student in the Soviet Union, studying at an institute of higher learning, was required to take a course called dialectic materialism, which was actually the study of atheism. The course was mandatory and was important because it required a passing grade in order for a student to continue with his or her studies. There was no theological faculty at this, or any other university, in the whole of the USSR. It was virtually impossible for a student to have access to any religious material in any positive form. So well was the media controlled and society structured under then party chief, Leonid Brezhnev and his grim-faced party apparachiks, that there was no danger of a student deriving a dissenting view on the question of the existence of God. The atheistic line taught by the educational institutions reigned supreme. There was to be no competition! The key issue in atheistic doctrine had been "solved." When asked by a professor as to whether God existed or not, a student could be relied on to answer intuitively, "There is no God!" The Soviet scientific apparatus had been skillfully harnessed to proclaim the non-existence of the supernatural.

The great monolith of the state had also gone to great lengths to weed out religion from society. Unless a church was registered and thus, tightly regulated, public religious services were banned. Contacts between Soviets and western tourists were fiercely monitored and controlled by the KGB and its millions of informers. The mass media regularly assaulted and scorned anything that sounded religious. No positive mention of God surfaced in any publications, except in the illegal samiztats (underground publications). Censors working at all levels of the official media were proud of their track record.

Actually, there was no debate for the Soviet student. The existence of God was not even an issue by the time one entered university. It was assumed that everyone knew that God did not exist. The government had to be commended for doing such a thorough job in exercising mind control on such a massive scale. All entry points into this giant Union of Soviet Socialist Republics, were tightly controlled. Upon entry, a tourist would be subjected to tight security, with his or her car, luggage, clothes, wallet, and often body, being searched. This was not for weapons, narcotics or profane literature, but for ideological "weapons" like the Bible or Sunday school materials for children. The goal was clear: to purge society of all reactionary tendencies to believe in religious "rot." The State believed that until their atmosphere was completely sterile, "danger" would lurk somewhere, unchecked, inside the parameters of this massive land. The hope was to allow the next generation to grow up in a pollution-free climate, where it would be almost impossible to come under any religious influence. It was in this way the youth of the land would be liberated from superstitious beliefs in an unseen world. The bottom line of Soviet ideology at that time in history was: We simply do not need God! We have found a better way! Years later, the stupidity of this line would become evident as Soviet Communist ideology lay belly up, bankrupt and in total desolation with its leaders searching for a belief system to give to its people.

The advocates of atheism had succeeded in plugging up every potential source of information from hungry, inquisitive students continually exploring new spheres of knowledge. There was only one "source" they had failed to silence. The families of those who had found a faith in the living God. Laura was one of them "at risk." She had a Christian mother who belonged to a group of active believers. And what an example her mother was.

Eva took a took a real interest in helping those who were suffering, something unusual in Soviet society. Frequently, she would bring home stinking alcoholics off the streets, and care for them. Drunk as skunks, they would pass out on the kitchen floor. Eva would wash their dirty faces and blood-stained hands. As they would eventually return to the "land of the living," Laura's mother would serve them hot tea and cookies as well as seasoned words about the God who loved "even drunkards." Laura was aware that the State could care less for these social dropouts of Soviet society. When Laura would return home from her studies, the stench from the kitchen would overpower her. With obvious contempt, Laura would ask her mother in Russian, the language they spoke at home, "Why do you have to bring these awful people into our home? Let the militia (police) take care of them. It is their job!" Her mother's response was swift. "Laura," she would say gently, "you do not yet understand what the love of God really is. Jesus died for these people. When God's love fills your heart, you cannot pass by a suffering person. You haven't yet experienced His love. But when you do, you will understand."

It was not long before Laura was forced to respond to the question of God's existence. To her fellow students, she seemed confident in her atheism, but Laura found a nagging uncertainty about her position creep into her mind. As she pondered her mother's righteous and unselfish life, Laura began to ask herself if her mother was "deluded," or if she really did believe in God. Of course, her mother must be wrong because the premise of Soviet science showed to any right-thinking person that there was no Supreme Being. Or was there? An unexplainable uneasiness set in. Perhaps, Laura thought, the debate is not over. Laura had yet to answer the great questions of life for herself. How did she come to be on this earth and why was she alive? Where was she going when she died? The bleakness of the atheistic doctrine that when one passed from this life, it was the end, seemed so pointless.

Laura's restlessness grew as she decided to carry out her own investigation with the resources available to her. On her bedroom table were stacks of books. In one heap, were textbooks and literature on atheism. By their side, with an opposing doctrine, lay only one book—mother's well-leafed Russian Bible. As Laura began to pore over the well-written textbooks, the logic she read appeared to be airtight. It was in tune with the world view of any "sensible" young student.

She decided that Christianity appeared to be prehistoric. Believers, she decided, resembled fossils, beings that had fallen behind the "enlightened" times.

Then Laura decided to investigate her mother's old and worn Bible. It contained no pictures, no graphs, charts or mathematical formulas. It seemed incredible to her that the message of this ancient book had survived the test of time, the fierce criticism of great minds over the millenniums. Laura asked herself why this book was so hated, so fiercely attacked and feared to the point that it had been largely outlawed in the Soviet Union and other Communist states. It was rather odd that bookstores did not carry such a book. Even more mysterious to her was the fact that the readers of the Bible were persecuted, interrogated, imprisoned and tortured. What, she asked herself, was it that caused such uncompromising faithfulness to the Bible's teachings and the God of her mother and millions of other followers of Jesus Christ?

Delicately, Laura picked up her mother's Bible. It fell open in the Book of Proverbs. Laura started to read the words before her and marveled at the wisdom it contained. She found it strange that the instruction and wisdom of life there before her eyes in the Proverbs, was missing from the textbooks on atheism. Next, the young inquisitive medical student stumbled across the book of Psalms. How beautifully, poetically and pointedly, the Psalmist had penned his message. Inexplicably, the Bible began to speak to her, even though Laura's intellect could not fully fathom the things she read.

The inner conflict in Laura's heart had brought her to a wrenching dilemma. Who was telling the truth? The Bible or the textbooks? The deepest recesses of her mind were turning into a confusing ideological battlefield. She had read that "scientific truths had disproved the antique foundations of the Bible." Evolutionary theories had blasted away at the righteous, God-fearing, lifestyle of her mother. The answer was not yet in sight. Both the Bible and the textbooks could not be true. One of them had to contain absolute truth. But which was it?

As she sat there at a small table by the Soviet-made rug that covered the central portion of the floor, under the flickering yellow light of a weak electric bulb dangling from the ceiling, Laura recalled how she had often returned from an evening at the theater or the movies and seen her mother on her knees. She was kneeling by her sofa-bed in the living room. She would tiptoe past her mother to her bedroom. As she did, she would witness her mother praying out loud, "Dear God, in the name of Jesus, please save Laura. Please save my child."

One prayer uttered in late September 1967, aggravated Laura. She wanted to roughly shake her mother and say, "Stop this right now! Don't pray like that. I do not need any salvation." But Laura loved her mother deeply and, although she did not appreciate the content of the prayer, she could not argue with the fact that each time her mother got up from her knees, her complexion spoke of something special that had just taken place. She radiated peace and happiness. So, what was it? Self-suggestion, psyching oneself into a frame of mind? Or was she actually talking to someone who was listening?

Unable to resolve the question that had formed in her mind, Laura finally decided she would try to pray herself. After all, what could she lose? If God did not exist, she would, at least, discover the truth. On this night, she sank to her knees beside her bed and began to talk to "whomever" was out there. "God," she began hesitantly, "if You are there, then let me know that You really exist. I am not asking for a supernatural miracle to prove your existence, but if You are there, You must see that I am at a decision point in my life right now. "If You answer me now, I will surrender my whole life to You, for Your service, because then I'll have nothing more worthy in the whole world than to serve the Living God, my Creator! But if You do not answer me now; if I do not receive the assurance that You are really there, then I will get up off my knees and go to the university and tell everyone there that You do not exist. I will never return to this question again, because I will know that when I prayed to You at the most important moment in my life, You never answered." There was a long silence. All Laura could hear was her heavy breathing. She stayed on her knees. War was being waged in the spiritual realm. It wasn't long before she received the answer she was waiting for!

Laura as a medical student before her expulsion from the university.

Laura (middle) with classmates.

Chapter Six

Land of the Reindeer

On that balmy summer's evening in 1971, it started out as just another regular Saturday night youth service at our church in Vancouver, B.C. We had begun by singing contemporary worship songs to the accompaniment of a band. Our new pastor, the Reverend Paul Kusmin, a Finn who had been working as a missionary in the East African nation of Kenya, had accepted a call to move out of the sunshine of Africa, to the more moderate climate of my adopted city. Pastor Paul was gifted in languages and was fluent in four, including Russian, but that night he spoke only in English. After a short, but powerful sermon, he called young people there who wanted to rededicate their lives to Jesus Christ to come forward.

Not really understanding what was about to occur, I walked to the front and knelt by the piano and the potted palm tree decorating the piano, closed my eyes and began to repeat the pastor's prayer of commitment. After I had completed the prayer, the pastor approached me and sank to his knees by my side. He then put his arm around my shoulder and began speaking out loud a prophetic prayer. "Hannu, God will send you into missionary work," he said slowly but firmly. "You will serve the Lord by winning souls for Christ in a far-away land."

I felt a surge of power shoot into my body. My mind flashed back to when the American evangelist had blessed me at the John Oliver High School, and now had come the pastor's prophetic prayer. I knew that God was reminding me of an upcoming time in my life that I, as yet, knew nothing about. Could it be true that God really had a plan for my life? Of one thing I was convinced. God was gently calling me, asking whether I was willing to serve Him. I felt that still, quiet voice saying to me as I knelt there, Will you give Me first choice in your life? Will you allow me to lead you the way I desire? I nodded my head as tears of joy began to fall down my cheeks. Why would God want to use someone like me? I could not answer that question, but I was totally aware that this was a turning point in my young life!

* * * * *

Bible school was not quite the in-thing for a 17-year-old student at Argyle Secondary High. My teenage years were filled with fishing for salmon in the crystal clear streams of British Columbia, wrestling on the high school team and riding big motor cycles.

"Hey, Hannu, there is a package for you from Finland," my mother announced as she leafed through the day's mail. "I guess it's that brochure you wrote for from that Bible college in Finland."

But by the fall of 1971, I was nearing the end of my studies in high school and I sensed that an approaching crossroads in my life was imminent. I had become aware that if I was to be a missionary, I needed to attend a Bible school where I could study God's Word in depth. The pastor had told me about a Bible school in southern Finland which was 65 miles north of Helsinki. I figured my schooling in Canada would not suffer too much if I took time off to go there. I knew I could continue my studies for an extra semester after returning.

So, along with three others from our church, Timo, Tarmo, and Mauri, I returned to the country of my birth for what proved for me to be a wonderful experience where I could join with others to learn about Him from His Word and also be alone with God and listen to His voice.

It was while at this Bible school that I experienced the infilling of the Holy Spirit, a time when I felt a warm wave of power descend on me. Hot, sticky tears flooded my eyes as I felt an unspeakable joy flood my whole body. It was a highly emotional experience for me. As I stepped outside the Bible school chapel, I spotted a group of students standing around and charged towards them and, not being able to contain my jubilation, blurted out what had just happened to me.

Standing outside, totally enveloped in a supernatural joy, I wanted to hug the whole world and shout, "Listen everybody! Jesus loves you! He died for you and wants to save you." A supernatural love possessed me from head to foot. I could feel God in every cell and sinew of my body. Now I comprehended how greatly God had loved the world when He sent his Son to die for our sins. As I stood in the freezing cold of that fall day in Finland, I shouted, "Dear God, I want to make you an offer. Here is my life. If You have any use for it, please take it. It's Yours. You have first choice. Do as You will. If You don't need me, then I will try to make use of my life in the best possible way. In any case," I continued as a lone woman shopper stood close by and fixed me with a bemused eye, "I will always love You and respect Your Word." I was very aware that God had heard my prayer. It was the very prayer He had been waiting to hear from the time He had called me to serve Him.

Yet, even after this memorable experience, I had access to no more information about God's plan for my life than before. For reasons only known to Him, He chose not to reveal His will more than one step at a time—but now I knew I did not have to understand the next step. I just had to be obedient to whatever He asked of me. I had enlisted in God's army and, as a private I just had to obey the orders. Mine was not to question anything — I just had to do it! But where, I pondered, would He ask me to serve Him on the frontlines? Russia was about the last place on my mind.

*****

BIOLOGY AND THE BIBLE

The Canadian School Board had successfully removed Bible reading and morning prayer from its public school system in the same way the United States did a little earlier. The School Board and the Ministry of Education in Canada could in no way be viewed as being at open war with religion. Equal rights for all regardless of religion or race was the ticket. Students, on the other hand, frequently ridiculed those who chose to believe in God, especially those who openly professed their faith.

Mr. Walker was an exception to the School Board. He was a tall, elderly man with spectacles, white hair and a white beard that all too well matched his white cloak. His outward appearance made him look like the model professor to the point that it was intimidating. Mr. Walker spoke English with a heavy British accent. He was to be my biology teacher.

It was my last year at Argyle Secondary High in North Vancouver. It felt a bit strange to be back in school after a six month break at Bible school in Finland. In the biology class we were set to study evolution, earth, life, species, and the fossil record.

Regardless of who got credit for the world I lived in, I loved nature and spent a lot of time outdoors. I liked biology even though there was a clear conflict between my religious convictions about the origin of the universe and the school textbooks. From day one, Mr. Walker seemed to be keenly aware of this conflict.

"Well, Hannu Haukka, please tell us what the Bible says about this? Where did these creatures come from?" said Mr. Walker referring to the very earliest life forms propagated by evolutionists as the earliest stage of man's evolution.

Strolling over to his book shelf he pulled out a King James version of the Bible and promptly marched over to my desk, laying it down in front of my face, open at a random spot. Mr. Walker had a smile on his face.

If there was still somebody in class who didn't know I was a Christian, they just found out.

Mr. Walker was three times my age. He had spent much of his professional life wading through the corridors of evolutionary thinking. He knew the school board (textbooks) material inside out. What was I compared to him? A sapling, totally unprepared for intellectual debate. The analytic thought patterns of a high school kid who had never been called on to defend his world view were no match for the so called "scientific evidence" crafted together by proponents of evolution and atheism.

From day one, students were taught to believe the establishment, the system. What teachers taught in school was considered the gospel truth. It was a WYTIWTB set-up. That stands for What You Teach Is What They Believe. If a child was taught there is no God, then there is no God. If one was taught that elephants are pink, then they are pink, until they actually see one for the first time. So, the teaching of evolution was "a matter of fact—no questions asked," sort of thing.

The theory of evolution was full of holes and missing links. Presentations were riddled with words like "possibly", "likely", "perhaps", "approximately", "for unknown reasons". I was too inexperienced as a debater to draw attention to the lack of persuasion in these words.

I had no response. I possessed no intellectual armor for a defense nor weaponry for an offense. There had been no forewarning of an imminent attack. I had come to school to learn, not to argue. My intellect couldn't counter Mr. Walker's arguments. Yet, my heart resisted him stubbornly.

The proposition that man had evolved from apes seemed ludicrous. Nebraska Man was the product of a tooth that later turned out to belong to an extinct pig. Piltdown Man's jawbone was found to belong to a modern day ape. Peking Man was said to be 500,000 years old although all evidence of his existence has disappeared. Then there was everyone's favorite. Neanderthal Man. His skeleton, it was announced at the 1958 International Congress Of Zoology, really belonged to an old man who had suffered from arthritis. A simple little comic book called "BIG DADDY" would have sent thundering shock waves through biology class had I had it at my disposal.

Documented results from scientific research would have blown the very foundations of the evolutionary theory sky high. Things like moon dust, the spin rate of the earth, the shrink rate of the sun.

*Moon dust accumulates at a rate of 14.3 tons every year. After 4-5 billion years the moon's dust layer should have been 140 to 300 meters thick. It isn't. It's 0.5 - 7.5 cm thick. What space broom could have swept the dust away?

*Atomic clocks measure a decrease in the earth's spin rate. Accordingly billions of years ago the earth would have spun so fast that it would have flung everything loose on the surface into space. How about trying to study evolution in a whirlwheel?

*The sun shrinks at a rate of 1.5 meters per hour. A scant 100,000 years ago the sun would have been twice the size it is today. Twenty million years ago the sun's surface would have touched the earth. Strange how Mr. Walker never mentioned such scientic data.

*Oh, not to mention the "source" of the information, the teleonomy in every living cell, making life possible. Evidence suggests that somewhere there is a "Programmer" who programmed the very life, the ordering principle of the living cell. The schoolboard suggested it all just came together randomly. No design, feat of engineering, technological advancement, no computer program, it just came together without an engineer, a designer, a programmer!

The evolution theory was full of holes. Any student passing the final exam had apparently memorized the biology textbook. To believe that man actually evolved from a primordial ooze and that his ancestors were once apes one had to be an absolute intellectual idiot. Alas, for me all the counter evidence came too late.

"The Bible presents an opposite view," I managed to say after a moment of silence while staring at the open Bible on my desk. That was the depth of my scientific argument.

The bombardment continued until the end of the semester. At the last lecture of the semester the teacher surprised both me and rest of the class. "What happens after a person dies?" queried Mr. Walker.

"We have studied where man came from. But what happens to him after he dies?" Mr. Walker examined his students through his glasses, lightly moving his upper teeth against the lower. "We haven't discussed that yet, have we? Is it all over when this bionic body is buried?" The class was silent. Mr. Walker was waiting for an answer. Nobody volunteered.

"Hannu, what does the Bible say?"

"I've ribbed Hannu all year long about God and the Bible. Let me say this. When it comes to the subject of death, I am inclined to believe as Haukka here does—the way the Good Book tells us. It's not all over when we die. There is something more..."

I was exhilarated. Was I hearing things? I literally tingled. How did he dare to cross over to my side? He'd been so cynical all year long.

After class was dismissed about half of the students came up to my desk, many of them smiling. "I just want you to know, that I too believe in God. You just had the courage to say it."

I found out later that some of the students since then had boldly professed their faith in God. Years later, they still remembered biology class and my exchanges with Mr. Walker.

* * * * *

The summer, fall and first winter back in Finland had gone fairly well for a guy reared in North America. Although I had been born in Finland, my being brought up in a Finnish immigrant family in Canada, wasn't enough to keep me Finnish. I was Canadian, and proud of it. So being back in Finland, in ministerial training, was an educational process for me to be immersed in another society and culture.

The political system in Finland was so different from Canada and the general attitude toward other races was different. Canada was a melting pot of all nations, while Finland was no where near that definition of racial coexistence. By and large, Finlanders were not receptive to coexistence with other races on Finnish soil—with the exception of the Swedish-speaking population in its coastal cities. But, even with the Swedes, there were a lot of prejudices. The Swedes were considered more rivals than neighbors. Finns in most cases made no secret of their negative views against its small Gypsy population, who could not hide their identity because of their darker complexion, dress, traditions and culture.

Finland was not my idea of an affluent society. The people had learned to live with less and do things differently than the people of Canada. Back home, I owned a 650 cc Yamaha motorcycle, but now I drove a borrowed 50 cc moped. Instead of a powerful rumble between my legs on the highway, I had to be content with the whine, and ring-a-ding pop-popping of the moped's struggling engine. Instead of living in my own bedroom, I slept on a narrow bed in a shared dorm at the Bible college. Instead of going to McDonalds or Burger King, I sparingly bought a wierd looking hot dog twice a week. Gleaming big American cars were a rarity, though there were Ladas, Skodas, VW Beetles, and some Saabs and Volvos. Finland, at that time, had no megastores, supermarkets or malls, just small shops.

In short, I had to do some radical adjusting to a new lifestyle and to learn the ways of a remote northern nation. Another difficulty for me to wrestle with was the Finnish winter with temperatures plummeting down to 40 degrees below zero, Celsius. There were extended periods of darkness from November to February. In Lapland, which is located in the northern part of the country, above the Arctic Circle, the sun would not rise at all for two, long months. Generally, there was also lots of snow, something we had little of in Vancouver, which had no winter to speak of. With the ocean alongside, temperatures seldom dropped there below freezing.

I did, however, admire the Finns for their adeptness at Arctic survival. The far north had conditioned them and it showed during the Second World War when winter was to the advantage of the Finnish Army as it fought off waves of attacking Soviet troops. The locks on the rifles of Soviet soldiers froze in record freezing temperatures. The Red Army forces were also poorly dressed for such severe conditions. This proved to be a catastrophe for the invading Russians.

By spring, the novelty of being in Finland began to wear off. I had seen all the tourists' attractions and I was no longer considered a guest from across the sea. Now was the time for me to work alongside the people to whom I ethnically belonged.

You could be forgiven for assuming that Finns are religious people. Statistics seem to point to an impressive role for the Lutheran Church in Finnish society. Almost nine in ten Finns are officially members of the church, 90 percent of babies are baptized, 92 percent of 15-year-olds are confirmed, and well over 80 percent of marriages take place in church weddings, while baptisms and funerals bring virtually the whole Finnish population into contact with the church every year. In schools, confessional religious teaching in accordance with the Lutheran faith, is an essential part of education. Schooldays usually begin with a religious assembly, and occasionally pupils attend a service in their local church. Despite all this, Finland—together with the other Nordic countries—forms one of the most secularized regions in the world.

The percentage of Finns belonging to the Lutheran Church has been decreasing for years, and those who leave the church generally stay outside of all religious communities. Only three percent of Finns belong to other denominations, mainly the Orthodox Church and the Pentecostal movement. It, however, wasn't my purpose to evangelize Finland. I was to return to home base in Canada for ministry there after my training.

As a trainee, I had illusions about the holiness and devoutness of the local pastors. As a boy, I had always looked up to ministers. I thought they were without fault, men who prayed endlessly, studied their Bibles in offices for eight hours a day and never cracked any jokes. It was not long before I realized that they were just as human as anyone else. In one case, I was with a group of preachers who pulled straws to see who would pay for morning coffee in a coffee shop. There were roars of laughter when the loser was identified. I also noticed that not all their talk was sanctified and without blemish. Yet, I thank God to this day that there were those whose example I could look up to. I viewed those men with great respect. They were honorable and I desperately wanted to be like them.

The novelty of my surroundings no longer occupied my thoughts. This left me free to ponder the meaning of my stay; my purpose of being in Finland. And a restlessness overwhelmed my spirit. I started to question the value of coming over. Was I really in God's will by staying in the country of my birth, brushing up on the Finnish language? One day, one of the leaders of the denomination I was serving, Eino Ahonen, a short, stocky bald man, stopped by the Bible college. He was the chairman of the denomination's publishing house based in Helsinki and also the leader of the denomination. "Hannu," he said as we talked, "you remember you took an excellent photograph of me when I was here last?" I nodded, recalling that I used a Nikon F SLR camera that I had purchased from a professional photographer back in Vancouver. "Well our present photographer is leaving and his post is now open," he said. "Would you like to take it?" Mr. Ahonen made it clear that it was a temporary position that I could hold until they could find a Finn to take over the job. So, I agreed to take it.

I was satisfied and challenged with my work for the first few months in Helsinki. I was in charge of all photography for the weekly and monthly magazines that the publishing house put out. I would also shoot pictures for their LP and cassette covers. In addition, I processed all the pictures that illustrated a Bible concordance and dictionary they were producing. My church back home had discontinued my monthly support as I was now on salary with the publishing house.

Summer passed by quickly with a flurry of activity. The chairman had forgotten all about the promise of finding a permanent photographer. I began to feel a deep uneasiness rise up inside of me. I reasoned that I had made a mistake. Here I was just slinging a camera on the streets of Helsinki. This had nothing to do with proclaiming the Gospel. It was in conflict with my original purpose for being in Finland. The age-old piece of wisdom, "A picture is worth a thousand words" gave me little comfort.

Six months of taking pictures, working in the dark room processing them, seemed a waste of time for me. I needed to get back to Canada and resume my life over there. The church in Vancouver had sent me to Finland for ministerial training. I had become a photo developer. That was the way I saw it.

To deal with this situation, I rapped on the door of Walter Luoto, the managing director of the publishing house. "Come in," said Walter, a man I guessed was between thirty-five and forty. "Oh, Hannu. It's you. Pull up a chair. What can I do for you?" I sat down across from his desk awash with papers, books from America that he was to read to see if they were suitable to be translated into Finnish. "Mr. Luoto," I began, "I am here to hand in my resignation." He peered at me over the top of his glasses, but said nothing, so I continued. "I came here to study the Bible, brush up on the language of my ancestors, share the Gospel with the Finnish people and then return home," I said testily. "I don't think photography is to be the challenge in my life and I can't justify doing only photography, so I would be grateful if you would release me from my position here."

He reluctantly accepted my resignation and I decided to pack my bags and book myself on a Canadian Pacific Air flight back home.

Just before leaving, I was walking along Mannerheim Street, the main street in the city center of Helsinki. The parliament, central post office and the Finlandia Concert Hall, were on this same street.

The light was still green at the intersection. I rushed onto the crosswalk on Mannerheim and Kaivo streets. But then I abruptly stopped in my tracks when I spied the familiar face of Raimo Grönroos, a freelance journalist studying history at the University of Helsinki.

"Hi there, Hannu," he said brightly. "I'm just on the way from a travel agency. I'm planning another trip to Russia with a small group to encourage the underground church there. Do you want to come along?"

Hannu in 1973, the year God called him to ministry.

Chapter Seven

Questions

The year was 1974 and, because of the October Revolution festivities, Russia's borders had been sealed tighter than a drum. Moscow's Red Square was used as a huge open-air theater for a glossy celebration of the might of the Soviet military with the latest hardware of mass destruction rumbling across the cobble-stones of the mighty square. Stonefaced Soviet leaders stood proudly atop the bulky Lenin Mausoleum in the crisp gold sunlight of autumn, relishing the glories of the awesome power that kept their empire intact.

Tanks, armored personnel carriers, rocket launchers rumbled by and infantry units marched in formation, followed by members of the Communist party waving red flags with the hammer-and-sickle and pictures of the holy trinity of Marx, Engels and Lenin, as well as the present leader, Leonid Breznev. It seemed that the Soviet system was a kind of pagan cult of religion.

The entire working class population of the Soviet Union was mobilized to join the massive outdoor parades in support of the Communist party. They had been well briefed about

48

which slogans of endorsement to the glories o
had to shout out and then they would sponta
into the singing of the national anthem.

As I watched on Finnish television this ma
of power through Red Square, the center of the S
and located along the east wall of the Kremlin, l
my stomach as it gave the impression that the wl   ..ion
fanatically believed in communism. I realized only too well
that many of them secretly knew that it was hostile ideology
that could only be sustained by fear.

From the very inception of communism, its ideologues
had understood that man was a religious being. He had a
mysterious, built-in tendency for worship.

He needed something to believe in, something to live for
and something valuable enough to die for. For the purposes
of communism, that something could not be the God of the
Bible, because that God did not share His glory with anyone
or anything. A nation that believed in God could not be ma-
nipulated. Unconditional faithfulness and obedience could not
be extracted from them.

So, instead of God they placed a new religion, with
Vladimir Ilyich Lenin, as their messiah.

It seemed to me that the Soviet system had cursed the
Russian people with a system that robbed them materially,
while impoverishing their spirit with deceit and corruption.

Western tourists were not allowed into the USSR at that
time because the October Revolution festivities were considered holy and only for those sympathetic to the cause of communism. Communists and Socialists from other countries,
including most Western nations, were invited to join in the
celebrations.

In addition, embassy representatives of foreign countries
were also present in Red Square to view the military parade
and to try and decipher the rhetoric of the following speeches
of party leaders.

All of this had caused our planned trip to be postponed
for a few days. I filled out my visa application at the travel
agency giving tourism as my reason for the visit. At that time,
it was really the only thing you could put into an application.

..cating the reason for my travel was to encourage members of Russia's illegal underground church, would have jeopardized their security.

Finally, our little group clambered aboard a green VW Kleinbus in Helsinki to head for the border crossing at Vaalimaa. It took a couple of hours and I felt my heart begin to pound as we stopped at the red-and-white pike pole manned by two Russian soldiers who solemnly examined our passports and then handed them back without comment. One of them told us to proceed to the inspection area a few hundred yards ahead.

"See those high watchtowers?" said Raimo. "They are manned by Soviet frontier guards equipped with automatic rifles and binoculars. This whole area is mined. There is next to no chance of escape."

In actual fact, the Soviet frontier zone was a buffer twenty miles deep with three separate barbed wire fences at various intervals. You had to cross them all to escape.

The border guards in the inspection area had German shepherd dogs with them and they were equally as intimidating as those at the pike. But their check of our documents and the vehicle was surprisingly cursory. We were finally in Russia.

Winter weather had arrived and darkness was soon enveloping us. Our van ploughed through the slush on the Leningrad highway, sending mud flying everywhere each time we hit a pothole. From time to time, I could make out the silhouette of the remains of an onion-domed church. To better see the road ahead, Raimo had switched on the headlights, something that peculiarly was not allowed in Russia. One was expected to drive on parking lights even on unlit roads. The sight of our headlights, provoked oncoming drivers to flash on their lights at us in disgust.

After about three hours, we arrived in Leningrad — the cradle of the 1917 revolution and headed for the Moscow train station, located in a large square building with a sharp, high, needle-like steeple perched on top of it. (There are four stations in the city.) Raimo parked the van in a guarded area near the Intourist office after which we were escorted to the train station and we headed onto the platform to catch the 21:34 PM night train to Petrozavodsk. Attached to the green carriages was a postal car, a restaurant car, and fifteen sleeper cars for passengers. There were no merchants selling goods outside the station or by the trains. It was strictly forbidden and punishable by law.

As we took our seats, I noted that the Russian passengers all had gray, expressionless faces that I guessed masked how they truly felt.

The train soon creaked forward and so began the overnight journey. The locomotive would frequently stop with a slam, bang and jerk, waking us up in our cots at different stations. We shared our compartments with several Russians. In mine there were four of us, two Finns and two Russians. As I did not yet speak Russian, I had been urged by Raimo to refrain from speaking in English or Finnish so as not to arouse unnecessary suspicion.

After an uncomfortable journey, the train finally arrived in Petrozavodsk at 7:30 a.m., exactly on time. As we stepped onto the platform, Raimo spotted Seppo, our Intourist guide who was waiting for us. In his forties, Seppo was of medium build, wearing a gray overcoat, gray fur hat and dark pants. He had been picked for us by the government tourist agency because he was fluent in Finnish.

After breakfast in the Hotel Pohjola, Seppo told us of the tour of the city a mandatory part of our itinerary. I decided to skip the tour and, instead go to the home of Laura, the young Christian whom I had met three years earlier, to let her know that we had arrived. I had a mental picture of where she lived and, with little trouble, I found the wooden two-story barrack-style building.

Nothing had changed since my last visit. The building had not been painted and the main entrance was just as shabby. The front door still swung loosely on its squeaky hinges. Laura and her mother lived on the ground floor at the very end of the building.

Hesitating for a moment to make sure I had the right door, I gently knocked. The door opened and there before me was Laura, her brown hair drawn back into a bun. I gasped as I saw what a beautiful young woman she had become. Her innocent blue eyes were pale like water diamonds, as she smiled her welcome. It was the most charming smile I had ever seen.

She was then twenty-nine years of age. As she signaled me to sit down on the sofa, Laura sat across from me and asked in heavily-accented Finnish about the reason we had come to her city.

"We wanted you and your fellow believers to know that you are not forgotten," I stammered, unable to take my eyes off her beautiful facial features. I wanted to tell her that we had also brought with us some Bibles and other Christian literature, but I found my voice had stopped working. A mustache of sweat was now on my upper lip.

Sensing my acute discomfort and seeing the brick red flush in my cheeks, Laura suggested she make a cup of tea for us to share. I tentatively sipped it as I gazed at her. I can hardly remember what else we talked about, though I did notice that a few curls had escaped the discipline of her bun.

I was in a daze. Was I falling in love with this young lady? Surely not!

Shocked at my own emotions, I stumbled back along the bleak streets of the city back to the hotel. That night I slept fitfully as Laura's face kept rising before me in my thoughts. I knew this was completely stupid. Laura was several years older than I, but even more of a problem was that she was a Soviet citizen. "No," I whispered to myself, "this could never work. There are too many roadblocks in our way."

I could hardly wait for the next morning. Our group were to attend an underground meeting in a log house that in no way resembled a place of worship. The inside was decorated with hand-painted pictures bearing Scriptures in Russian such as, "We preach Christ crucified."

About forty people were assembled. The men were dressed somberly in dark, two-piece suits and black shoes. I noticed that none of them wore ties—their tradition dictated that this was a vanity—and the top buttons of their white shirts were fastened. The women wore scarves covering their heads, in accordance with the Apostle Paul's instruction in the book of Corinthians.

The service was held in Russian and translated into Finnish, but I watched in wonderment as Laura confidently translated the proceedings into both languages for the sake of those who only spoke one.

The preacher then invited each one of us who had come from Finland to step to the front and bring a few words of greetings. When my turn came, I felt extremely nervous, partly because I was speaking publicly for the first time in Russia, but also because I had been warned by Raimo that there would almost certainly be a KGB informant in the service who was monitoring the proceedings and would then report them to his superiors. I did not want to say anything that would provoke my arrest and, more importantly, cause more difficulties for the gathered believers.

With Laura interpreting my words into Russian, I said in Finnish, "Our brothers and sisters in the West send you their fraternal greetings." I gazed out at the sea of wrinkled faces before me whose expressions told of trial, difficulty and trouble. "They pray for you, knowing how much hardship you are going through in your witness for Christ," I continued. "They admire your courage and steadfastness."

As I briefly then gave my testimony about what Christ meant in my life, I noticed smiles begin to light up their faces. Many of those sitting on benches in this church had been fined, threatened, arrested and some had even been in prison for their faith. What could I say to these people who were living out their faith in such trying circumstances?

Finally, I swallowed deeply, and said, "I am challenged this morning to live more for Jesus Christ because of your example." I sat down feeling cheap and hollow, yet God appeared to have blessed them through my simple words of love.

After the service, our group went to Laura's home for tea and cake. There were no cars to take us there, so we walked. It was not far away by Russian standards—only three miles. As we walked briskly, buses and trucks passed by, belching black smoke, and a few Ladas chugged by.

"Let's now go over to see my cousin Vera," suggested Laura. "She has played a large role in my upbringing."

The walk along the beat-up streets of the city, took about twenty minutes. As we stepped out in the freezing air, Raimo slipped alongside me, so I decided to ask him some pointed questions about Laura, who was some way ahead, leading the pack.

"I know she is still single, Hannu," he revealed, "but I also know that there have been several suitors from the West who have wanted to marry her and take her out of Russia."

Raimo said that none of these friendships had ever worked out. "To my knowledge, she doesn't ever want to leave Russia. Why do you ask?"

My faced again flushed with embarrassment. He got the message. "If you want my humble opinion, I think someone ought to save Laura from these awful conditions," he chuckled. "Why don't you ask her if she would ever consider leaving this country," he suggested helpfully.

Little did I know at the time was that Laura was not looking for a savior from the West. Her ministry among her fellow Russians was everything to her. She did not need any other goal in life. If she was ready to give up her studies and sacrifice her future because of her faith in God, she certainly was prepared to stay in her country for God's purposes.

After a short stay at Vera's home, we all headed for another meeting. The service became a blur for me as I kept my eyes firmly fixed on Laura as she confidently translated again from Finnish to Russian.

It was by now late Sunday afternoon, and the train back to Leningrad would be leaving in a matter of hours. I could not stop thinking about Laura. Had someone asked me for a weather report, I would have responded, "She has a sunny smile." There was no doubt about it. I was in love!

I desperately sought for an occasion to speak to Laura alone. But then, what could I say? How could I begin? She probably had not even noticed me and I was devising a plan to propose to her. It was plain folly on my part.

Here I was, a young man from Canada who had only been in town for two days, wanting to propose to this beautiful young woman. Where was I supposed to take her? Finland? Canada? What would be the purpose of her leaving? To minister to emigrant Russians? It also seemed impossible that she would ever be allowed out of Russia. No, it did not make sense.

I again revealed to Raimo my innermost thoughts. "You know, Hannu, it is awfully risky to propose to a girl after only seeing her for a couple of days," he told me as we stood in the street outside of Laura's apartment.

Despite his warning, my heart kept telling me that time was running out. I would be aboard the train in a couple of hours. Laura was beautiful and I had to clear up this matter. I gulped deeply and said out loud, so that Raimo could hear, "One, two, three. Jesus help me!"

I moved up beside Laura who had not yet gone in. "Could you remain behind for just a minute?" I said. "I have something I want to tell you."

There we stood and Laura gazed at me waiting for my important message. "Well, I uh...," I stammered as I tried in vain to find an opening line. An expression of bewilderment spread over Laura's face. "Yes, you see ..., well, what I want to say is..." Laura shot me a quizzical glance and then broke into a wide smile. She seemed to be amused with my awkward efforts to try to tell her something. Finally, something rational came out. "Laura", I blurted, "would you be willing to consider coming to the West? I mean . . ." The words "marry me" finally emerged from my lips.

There was a long, unsettling silence. Her eyes became distant as she reflected on my questions. Then she responded, "Do you want me to give you an answer right away?"

I took that to be a negative sign. "No, no hurry!" I interjected. "Think about it. Take your time. No problem. Don't rush! I can wait." Any other response was better than "No."

We went to Vera's house for a final cup of coffee before heading off to the train station. I felt confused as Laura joined the others in the room, laughing and talking as if nothing had happened.

I wondered how normal it was for a woman not to accept a proposal on the spot. At least she had not said "No." For that I was thankful. A "No" would have been devastating to me. There is still hope, I comforted myself.

It was time to move on. Our group put on our overcoats and hurried back to the Hotel Pohjola to fetch our luggage and passports, which had been held at the front desk, a normal custom at that time.

We attended an evening service, which had been similar to the one we had been at in the morning. Again it was a moving and emotional experience for me.

* * * * *

Some fifteen well-wishers had gathered at the station. They shook hands with us. I was taken aback when one of the men came up and kissed one of our group on the mouth. This was an honored Russian custom, but took me by surprise. Women also kissed women. Soviet believers quoted the Apostle Paul who said, "Greet each other with a holy kiss." I was later told that the more you were honored, the more kisses you got— three being the maximum.

I looked around for Laura and she was there, but was surrounded by her friends. I tried to wave out of the window as the train began to lurch forward to a shuddering start. A sense of sadness swept my whole being.

My heart was being left behind in Petrozavodsk.

Chapter Eight

Holy Spirit Hijack

I gingerly rapped on Walter's door. A green light came on the indicator panel signaling that he was free. "Come in," he shouted from inside as I opened the door. It was like a rerun of my previous visit to him just before I had left for Petrozavodsk. But now I had to swallow my pride and try to persuade him to let me stay.

I was soon to realize how God had strategically positioned me as a photographer at the publishing house. The publisher would allow me to travel to Russia and not risk losing my job and my salary was just large enough to cover my travel budget. I also understood that Helsinki was the best place for me to apply for my visa for repeated visits to Russia. It was God's perfect plan.

Even my strange accommodation in a bomb shelter, did not seem so bad now. The shelter consisted of three separate chambers sealed off by a main entrance with two heavy metal doors on hinges. The shelter—every building in Finland had to have one for the protection of employees in case of an air attack—had no furniture except for a piano, a few microphone stands, chairs, music stands. It was used as a recording studio for all albums released through the publishing house.

I slept on a foam rubber mattress that I laid out each night and rolled up in the morning. The soundproofing was so good that I don't think a tank battle within fifty feet of the building, would have woken me up. But thoughts of Laura did! I now had to stay in Finland to be near her.

"Hi Hannu," said Walter. "Did you have a good trip?" "That's what I needed to talk to you about," I began falteringly. "It worked out better than I ever would have thought. Is that photographer's post still vacant? If so, I'd like to apply for it." I could see from the quirky expression on his face, that he thought I had taken leave of my senses. So I explained the situation. Walter apparently understood the whole story without me explaining it to him. "You mean you now cannot leave for Canada, at least not until you hear from her," he said as he let his hands fall flat on his desk.

Walter revealed that he knew Laura. "She has acted as a translator for me during my visits to Petrozavodsk and also when I was at Joseph Bondarenko's church in Riga. She is certainly a lovely young lady." He said that many of the leaders of the denomination also viewed Laura as a kind of "hero of the faith" because she had given up her future as an eyesurgeon so she could, instead, serve God.

My boss leaned back in his chair, a half smile on his lips. "The job is still open!" he chuckled. "Do you want it?"

I canceled the air ticket back to Canada.

* * * * *

Night after night in my bomb shelter, I turned restlessly. I would then lie on my back, staring up at the dark. I kept wondering what Laura's response was going to be. It was now February 1975, three months after I had proposed to her, I still had not had a response. A peculiar foreboding began to hang over me and nothing was able to alleviate this strange nervousness I felt.

Unable to bear it anymore, I got off my mattress at about 3:00 a.m. one night, put on some warm clothing and made my way to a side entrance of the building. I gasped as the freezing night air struck me full force in the face. I walked outside and under the pressure of my feet the snow squeaked, verifying that the temperature was at least 15 degrees celsius below zero.

I knelt in the snow beside the building and prayed, "Lord, if You give me Laura, I will take it as a sign that You want to take my life and use it for Your purposes in the Soviet Union. I promise You my life!"

* * * * *

I sat comfortably in my seat in the Kallio (Rock) Lutheran Church, a huge cathedral-like building perched on a rock on a high hill overlooking the center of Helsinki. It was hewn out of gray stone slabs and had a huge steeple like a citadel that could be seen from miles away.

I had breathlessly walked up the steep hill to get to the church so I could meet the Reverend Earl Poysti, the international guest speaker of the night. Poysti was unquestionably the best-known radio evangelist in the Soviet Union at that time. I sat enthralled in my pew as I heard this giant of radio evangelism, share story after story of God's miracles as a result of the broadcasts he was involved with. "I compare the rod of Moses with a radio microphone," he declared.

I had made a study of the incredible way Poysti's broadcasts had impacted people within the Soviet Union. There were now thousands of "radio churches" scattered throughout the eleven time zones of the USSR. These were remote areas that had no church so a small group of believers would gather in homes, have an act of worship and then timed the end of the worship period to coincide with Earl Poysti's sermon. He had become the radio pastor to millions of Soviets.

Besides hearing the Reverend Poysti speak, I also wanted to convey to him a message from a man I had met during my visit to Petrozavodsk. In his thirties, this man lived in a small central Russian village about 700 miles east of Petrozavodsk. He happened to be visiting Laura's city and wanted to find an evangelical gathering of believers where be hoped there would be visitors from the West.

As a last resort, the man asked a militiaman, of all people, for directions. The officer knew of Laura's church and gave him directions. When the man arrived, the benediction had already been pronounced and we were all about to leave. Dressed in a sports jacket with a brown sweater underneath, he rushed up the center aisle to the front where our Western group were gathered. His rosy-cheeked face like the bright summer sun. Streams of tears ran down his cheeks.

As Laura had translated to Finnish from his breathless Russian, I understood him to say, "Some time ago, I was sitting at home listening to my radio. I was scanning the frequencies looking for an international station. Suddenly, I came across a strange program that I had never heard before. The language was familiar. It was Russian. But the songs I was hearing were different. I had never heard such beautiful music before. Then the speaker talked about things I had never heard of in all my life. He was speaking about God, who loved man so much that He gave His son to die in man's place on a cross."

The man, whose simple features and sincerity captured my interest continued. "During that thirty-minute program, I became convinced that God was real and that He loved me," he went on. "I knew I was a sinner and needed His forgiveness. At the end of the program, the speaker asked that anyone who wanted to join him in prayer to kneel by the radio. I got down on my knees before the radio receiver and opened my heart to God and I was born again right there and then."

The man took out his handkerchief and wiped further tears of joy from his eyes and added, "That's not all. The next evening, my wife as well as my father and mother were listening with me to the same radio program in our home. At the end of the broadcast, the speaker again began to pray. It was wonderful. My wife, my father and my mother, all knelt by the radio and invited God into their lives, just I had done."

I found it hard not to join in weeping with this dear man. He then told of eight neighbors and friends coming into his home to also listen to the program. "Every one of our neighbors and friends also got on their knees and accepted the Lord into their lives. "I don't know if there are other believers in our village, but I know there are twelve people who gather regularly to worship and praise God in our home."

"Oh, by the way the radio preacher's name was Earl Poysti," he declared. "When you go back," said the man, "please give my greetings to Mr. Poysti. Thank him and ask him if it would be possible to increase the programming. It is so needed in this country."

After he had completed his story, the Russian gave each of us a bone-crushing Russian bearhug. I will never forget his tear-soaked cheeks pressing against mine. Every cell of his body proclaimed his happiness and joy.

* * * * *

The service in the Finnish church was finally over and I was able to move to the front of the church to give Earl Poysti this man's greetings. At the same time, I decided to make the best possible use of the opportunity. "Brother Poysti," I said, "I need your advice. I am a young man who is madly in love with a girl from the Russian underground church who has been expelled from university because of her faith."

Poysti stared at me through his thick eyeglasses, but said nothing. "Brother," I asked, "could I get her out of the country? What could I do to help speed up the process?" The radio preacher finally responded. "Trust the Lord, Hannu," he said. "If it is God's will, everything will work out fine." That was the full extent of his advice.

Earl Poysti wanted to know more about Laura and her studies at the university. He seemed to be impressed with what I had told him. "Hannu, if Laura ever comes out to the West, I'd be happy to welcome her to join our family team in the radio outreach," he declared. "We have a real shortage of people as well qualified as she apparently is."

When the conversation was over, I casually looked to my left and right to see if friends were present in the same meeting. Suddenly, a familiar face entered my field of vision. There was Seppo, the leader of a team of Finnish Christians who was supposed to be in Riga meeting Laura. I also spotted Anya, his wife who was with him. A sense of panic swept over me.

"Why are you here?" I asked. "You're supposed to be Riga." All the color had drained from Seppo's face. I could see he was searching for words. Then it all came spilling out, "We were arrested in Riga. All the books we took in were seized. We were expelled from the country. We've just arrived back in Helsinki and decided to come straight here."

I listened in stunned silence. Laura, I thought, where was she when all of this happened? Soviets are not exiled when accidents like this occurred. I knew better than that.

"What about Laura?" I could scarcely breathe. Seppo was evidently aware of our relationship.

He looked at me with a deep sorrow in his eyes. "The last I saw of her was when she was taken out by the militia. She's been arrested!"

Chapter Nine

A Tail In Riga

It had been a quiet morning so far for Vladimir Lusanov in the Komitet Gosudarstvennoy Bezopastnosty, also known as the KGB (Committee for State Security) headquarters in Riga, a grim, three-story stone building that struck fear in the hearts of all who passed by it. He had read both Pravda and Isvestia from cover to cover and was wondering what else he could do to occupy the next few hours of his time in the office when his idle thoughts were interrupted by the insistent ringing of the phone.

"Hello," he rasped into the instrument as he inhaled deeply on his cheap cigarette, blowing out a cloud of gray smoke so that it snaked slowly up towards the ceiling and hung there like a rain cloud over a tropical island.

"Vladimir, this is Viktor from Petrozavodsk," said a muffled voice down the phone line.

"Hello comrade," said the Riga man, stubbing out the nub of the cigarette into his coffee cup. "What can I do for you?"

"Vladimir, I wonder if you would watch out for a young woman called Laura who has just left here on a flight for your city. She is a Christian and we believe she is going to make contact with some tourists from Finland who we suspect are carrying anti-Soviet propaganda [a term used by the KGB for Bibles]."

"Could you get one of your boys to meet the flight at the gate at the airport and then put a tail on her?"

The KGB officer then supplied a full description of Laura.

"Thanks for the tip, comrade," said Vladimir as he replaced the receiver with a satisfied smirk. After running his long fingers through lank, black hair, he said to himself as his spirits began to rise, "Vladimir, my boy, it looks like it's not going to be such a boring day after all."

* * * * *

The rendezvous in Riga, the capital of Soviet Latvia, between the Russian believers and the Finns had gone smoothly. The Finnish group had succeeded in smuggling in many Bibles, New Testaments and hymnals. Laura had been instrumental in this operation. She had flown the two-hour journey to Riga by a Russian turboprop. She was the strategic link between the East and the West as a liaison and translator ensuring that there would be no communication problems.

For Laura and many other Russian believers, traveling was a far from a simple task. She had now left university and was working a menial job at the "Svetlana" semiconductor plant in Petrozavodsk. Her every step was monitored by Mikhail Grigorievich, her foreman. He would report her every absence to the KGB who, once alerted, would put tabs on her movements. Because of the Finns and the importance of their mission, Laura had to find a way to obtain a leave of absence without arousing suspicion. In this case, Laura decided to use a tactic that was hard to monitor. She went to the local clinic to donate blood. Workers wishing to do so were entitled to a day off work.

Laura did not notice the man in a heavy trenchcoat standing in a haze of cigarette smoke in a small crowd of people milling around the gate as she emerged from the plane into Riga Airport. It had been a short flight to the capital of the Latvian Soviet Socialist Republic from her home city. After her internal passport had been inspected by a security officer, Laura headed outside and caught the bus into the downtown area of this city which stands at the head of the Gulf of Riga, an arm of the Baltic Sea, on both banks of the western Dvina River. To Laura, Riga was like a second home.

She was familiar with the rendezvous points in this city which has maintained the atmosphere of a medieval German city. It was to be a busy street close to the Doma Cathedral, built about 1215. This would provide the best possible cover. It wasn't long before she met up with Olga, a local Christian who was of medium build and slim.

They furtively embraced, both looking around to see if they had been observed. They didn't see anyone that was showing an undue interest in them, so they felt free to talk.

"Our friends from Finland should be here at any moment," said Olga, her face breaking into a wide grin. "Once contact is established, I'll escort them with the load of 'manna' to a secret unloading location."

Laura's main role in the plan was to be the interpreter between the Finns and Olga, who spoke only Russian. It looked like the plan was going to work like a charm. Laura could have a quick cup of tea at Olga's apartment before the evening service with her fellow believers in the city—another high point in her visit.

* * * * *

Seppo and his wife, Anja, had got off to a good start with their smuggling exercise. Soviet customs had not detected the precious load of Bibles and other books they had on their bodies bound in gauze to their backs, stomachs and legs. By that time Soviet customs had gotten wise concerning books hidden in luggage. Seppo and the group knew this. They had made the visit to Riga to help supply Russian Bibles, which were in short supply in the Soviet Union, as well as New Testaments, song books and concordances. In many churches, there was only one Bible. The pastor would read from it during the services, but he would read slowly so that members of the congregation could write down the text in notebooks they had brought with them. In this way, believers could accumulate a valuable collection of handwritten portions of the Bible which they could read over and over again once they got home. Over a period of years, some had even copied the whole Bible, while others had to be satisfied with the New Testament.

The Finns spotted Olga and Laura and headed in their direction. They dropped the bags which were quickly picked up by the girls who told them to follow them to the home of an elderly Christian couple who had courageously agreed to the books being stored in their fifth-floor apartment. They hadn't noticed that they had fallen under the scrutiny of State Security. The KGB were conducting war on an invisible front.

The stopover was brief. Just long enough to unload the literature. "Thank you so much," said Olga, as she signaled the four of them to leave.

Descending the stairs of the gloomy stairwell, they dodged two men in civilian clothing who pushed past them and began ascending the same staircase. For a brief moment, a sensation of fear swept Laura's being. Quickly she brushed it aside, labeling it as unnecessary paranoia. She thought she had seen one of the men at the airport.

Still a small voice inside tried to make itself heard. Something is dreadfully wrong, she thought she understood the voice to say. The group headed for Olga's apartment, which they reached after a brisk walk of about fifteen minutes. The Finnish guests, who were blithely unaware of the crisis that was brewing, were ready for a warm cup of tea after a busy late morning.

They gazed around the sparse room, furnished with a kitchen table and four chairs as well as a large wardrobe. On the wall was a poster with the inscription from Revelation 3:20, "Behold I stand at the door and knock..." The four of them chatted, sang the great hymn, "How Great Thou Art" with gusto and generally fellowshipped with each other.

"Let's have a picture together," suggested Seppo, as he produced his camera. He quickly snapped a photograph of his wife with Olga and Laura.

Suddenly, the doorbell buzzer came to life. Laura felt her heart sink as Olga rose from her seat and went to the front door.

"Militia!" The word shot into the room like an intruder. Laura froze with her cup of half-drunk tea in her shaking hand. "We want to ask some questions."

Olga could do nothing to stop the men as they roughly barged past her and came into the living room. Laura recognized one of them as being the man at the airport. She knew he wasn't militia, but KGB. Cold chills shot down her spine as he began firing questions at the four of them.

"Who are these people?" he snarled at Olga, pointing at the three of them sitting in a state of shock on a sofa.

Before she could reply, he interjected, "Which one is the interpreter?"

"That's me," volunteered Laura.

"You're coming with us," he exploded. "Gather up your belongings."

Laura thought quickly. "Don't confess anything or sign any piece of paper they give you," she told the couple in Finnish.

As she spoke, the KGB man roughly grabbed her and dragged her to the waiting police car, its lights flashing.

Olga was then arrested by the other man and taken to the same police car and pushed into a back seat with Laura.

The Finnish guests were about to be granted the honor of sharing in the sufferings of the persecuted church. The so-called war stories of Bible smugglers were about to become a reality to them. The arresting officers would have put Seppo into a separate vehicle had it not been for violent protests by Anja. In the end, all four Finns were squeezed into the one vehicle.

Instead of being taken to the KGB headquarters, the Finns were driven to the Hotel Riga where further questioning took place. An Intourist representative informed them that they would be expelled. They would be put on the night train to Leningrad where the interrogations would continue.

Laura and Olga were then taken to the KGB offices in Riga. The Finns had no idea what their fate would be.

Seppo and Anja were put in separate compartments so that they could not communicate with each other.

The train arrived in Leningrad on time. At the Astoria Hotel, Seppo was separated from the group. This was the very hotel where Adolph Hitler, having laid siege to Leningrad, had planned to hold a grand reception party after crushing the remaining resistance to his advancing war machine. Hitler's mid-winter siege in 1940 of Leningrad had lasted for 500 days and had ended in humiliating defeat for his forces at the hands of the Red Army. He had even preprinted a program for the reception, but it was not to be.

What had caused great suspicion for the KGB was the fact that Seppo and Anja had driven to Leningrad by car and then taken the train to Riga. This was most unusual for tourists from the West.

"So, you're guilty of bringing anti-Soviet literature into our country," the KGB interrogator growled in a heavy voice as he sat across a table in the hotel Intourist office.

"Nothing of the kind," responded Seppo. "I have broken no laws. Your constitution guarantees freedom of religion. So what have I done wrong?"

In another room, Anja was also under fire. "How was the literature brought into the country?" demanded the officer. Before she could answer, he continued firing questions in staccato fashion. "Where did you get the literature from? Who financed your trip? Do you cooperate with Western organizations?"

Anja's head began to spin as the questions came thick and fast from her male interrogator. Suddenly, she snapped. She could take it no longer and began to cry. In a rare act of kindness, the man picked up a cup and filled it with water from a nearby samovar and offered it to her.

"Thank you," was all she was able to stammer.

After gulping down the contents, Anja recovered her composure. "You wouldn't believe me if I told you," she said. The officer's tactics had begun to lull her into a false sense of security, so she confessed to her part in the operation. Lifting up her blue overcoat, she showed the man how she had been able to conceal a relatively large amount of the literature in secret compartments.

Anja, like many other Bible smugglers had struggled with the ethics of smuggling. The Bible has instructed all Christians to obey the law, but did that apply to laws made by an atheistic nation? Anja had recently decided before leaving Helsinki that, "We must obey God rather than man." Seppo, too, had resolved the issue by asking himself whether he had the moral right to deny a starving man his "bread." In question was the "bread of life" and millions in Russia were spiritually starving to death.

The officer handed Anja a pen and paper and asked her to write out "in her own words" what had happened. "You need to specify why you have committed this hostile anti-Soviet action," he stated.

Marshaling her strength, she took the pen and began writing. "I love the Soviet people," she began. "Therefore, I have brought this literature into the country." The KGB officer seemed satisfied with her partial "confession" and took the paper from her.

The ordeal was also over for Seppo. The two were reunited and a KGB officer delivered a final speech to them both.

"You have violated Soviet law," he said firmly. "You will be expelled from the country. You will be denied entry to the Soviet Union in future except for the one who has cooperated by confessing to her deed." That was Anja.

* * * * *

Back in Petrozavodsk, Laura's mother Eva read the telegram from Helsinki with mounting concern. It read, "How is Laura? Greetings, Anja."

Eva knew immediately that something was wrong. Her daughter had not returned home on the scheduled flight.

Some twenty-four hours earlier, about one thousand miles away, Laura was sitting in KGB headquarters with Vladimir Lusanov. "I want you to describe in writing the chain of events in chronological order," he hissed, pointing to a pen and paper in front of her. His face was taut and angry.

"I'm not going to write anything for you," asserted Laura hoarsely as her voice trembled with emotion. "I'm tired. "It's late." It was already 3:00 AM. "All normal people are asleep at this time," she responded defensively.

He put his face close to hers and examined the defiant face in front of him.

"You will not be allowed to leave before you have given us a written report," said Lusanov, his face reddening with contempt, as he lit up another cigarette and inhaled until his nose and lungs were thoroughly corrupted with the smoke.

Laura knew her interrogator meant exactly what he had said. To him, it made no difference whether she sat in his office for an hour, a week or a year. Time had no meaning in his line of business.

Laura saw the situation differently. She knew her mother would soon realize something had gone wrong and would be worrying herself sick. She would have to call the plant and explain her daughter's absence from work, not to mention the unavoidable "appointment" Laura would have with the security police in Petrozavodsk.

"Okay," said Laura finally as she felt a little more of her strength drain away. "What is it that you are interested in?"

"The Finns," said Lusanov triumphantly as his thin lips were pulled into a smile. "Where did you meet each other? What was the purpose of the meeting?" He began to wave a finger yellow with tobacco strains. "Who were they supposed to meet in Riga? For whom was the literature meant?"

Laura knew only too well that the literature was to go to Joseph Bondarenko, a pastor who had already served three terms in the prison camps of Russia. Joseph, who was born in Kirovograd, Ukraine in 1936, led an underground church in Riga and his congregation had rallied to Laura's aid when she, as a "babe in Christ" had encountered her first persecution. They had prayed for her and written letters of encouragement to help her through her difficulties. So Laura knew that if she was to confess everything, the consequences for the church and Joseph, in particular, would be catastrophic.

Joseph's parents were believers and in 1955, he felt challenged by God to reach the youth of the Soviet Union with the Gospel. He served his first pastorate in an unregistered church in Odessa in 1961. From there he moved to Kirovograd and on to Suhumi on the shores of the Black Sea. From there Joseph moved to Riga.

"Any questions pertaining to others I will leave unanswered," she told her interrogator as he let out a wide yawn. "I will respond to questions regarding myself, and that's all. What would you like to know?" Laura asked, her eyes by now red-rimmed from lack of sleep.

Vladimir glanced at his watch. He blinked as he saw that it was now 5 AM. "Well, I guess you've given me enough for the time being," said the KGB officer. "You are ordered to leave the city and catch the first train to Petrozavodsk."

Then, pointing to the array of confiscated literature, he added, "This material will be sent to the KGB in your city as evidence to be used against you at your trial. Our colleagues in Petrozavodsk will take this matter to its final conclusion."

As Laura got up to leave, Lusanov gave her his parting words. "Yes, young lady, five years in prison is a long time," he intoned. "You could have avoided it. You have chosen the road of suffering."

His face then contorted into an evil smile. It had been a good night fighting for "peace."

Chapter Ten

The Telephone Call

My right hand shook uncontrollably as I picked up the telephone at my desk in the publishing house in Helsinki and called the travel agency. That night had been the longest of my life as I tossed and turned waiting for the dawn to arrive.

"Hello," said the friendly voice at the other end of the line. The elderly lady worked for a travel agency that specialized in travel to the Soviet Union.

"Hello," I responded. "I need to book the first available trip to Petrozavodsk. Can you help me?"

"Of course," the lady said reassuringly. "Two weeks and your papers should be ready."

"Two weeks," I uttered bleakly. "Couldn't you speed things up a little?"

"I am sorry, Hannu," the lady pressed on, sensing my desperation. "You know how the East is. The Soviets do everything at their own speed—which is always slow!"

I mumbled my thanks, put down the receiver and sat there devastated. I then began to wrack my brains. What could I do to try and discover what had happened to Laura? Was she already in prison? Perhaps she has been tortured? I had to find out.

I brooded over the problem. I had one option. Although Laura did not have a phone in her home, I could book a so-called "messenger call." This was actually a telegram requesting the other party to come to the local telegraph office, which was usually open around the clock, where there was a bank of telephones for public use.

I was aware that all international calls were monitored by the KGB, but if Laura responded by showing up at the telegraph office, that would indicate to me that she was still free.

"Your call should come through in exactly forty-eight hours," said the helpful Finnish clerk at the Helsinki Postal and Telegraph office. "Be here on time or you will miss your call."

For the next two days, I tried to devise a contingency plan should Laura not respond, but nothing materialized.

I was at the office for the call with time to spare and I stood by the counter eyeballing the clock on the wall.

I jumped as a woman shouted from behind a counter a few yards away, "Petrovzavodsk is standing by. Go to the booth on your extreme right, please."

Beads of perspiration knotted my brow as I picked up the phone.

"Hello, this is Laura," said the soft voice down the line.

"Laura," I almost shouted. "Thank God, you are home. I thought you would be in prison by now."

She did not respond to my words, but said, "It's all in the hands of the Heavenly Father."

By now, I was choking back the tears as I listened to Laura's voice. I was not aware that she was expecting a summons from the KGB any day, but I did know that she needed me at her side. I told her that I would be in Russia as soon as possible.

"Could you meet me in Petrozavodsk?" I asked.

"I'm not sure," she said. Her parting words were, "It depends on what they decide..." With that, the phone line went dead and I replaced the receiver with tears welling up in my eyes. I wiped my eyes with a handkerchief and headed out into the street. "They" must have meant the security police in her home town, I reasoned.

* * * * *

As I anxiously waited for the visa and tickets for my trip back into Russia, many uncertainties began to surface in my mind. More than six months had passed since I had proposed to Laura. I still had not received a reply from her and I knew that there must be something that was causing the uncertainty in her spirit. The arrest in Riga had compounded the situation. Gray despair filled my heart, and agonizing days began to shred away like the morning mist.

I would lie awake on my bed in the bunker and go over the problems we faced. What if Laura was sentenced to prison? Would I be there in five years to meet her at the prison gates? On the other hand, if she was not sentenced, what would be the chances for her to be given permission to leave Russia? Even before the events in Riga, those chances appeared to be slim.

I jumped as the phone rang in my office. It was the travel agent. "I have your ticket and visa to travel to Petrozavodsk," the woman informed me. "Could you come and collect them?"

Could I?

* * * * *

Contrary to the KGB prediction in Riga, I did go and meet Laura. State security in Petrozavodsk had mysteriously fallen silent. It seemed that they were patiently waiting to make their next move.

As the ferry ploughed through the Gulf of Finland from Helsinki towards Tallinn, Estonia, on my next trip, I prayed that God would "have His will" with our relationship. I tried to come up with something that I could say to Laura if she was still undecided about marriage. I felt the Lord encouraging me to "Remember Gideon." Gideon, in the Old Testament, had put out a "fleece" for the Lord to determine His will. Wet or dry, the fleece would be a sign to him.

As I sat on board the ship on August 1, 1975, as it swayed gently back on forth, I again I felt the Lord say something to my spirit: "Hannu, if the plan to be married is of Me, then get Laura to apply for a visa to come to Finland for a visit." The matter was settled.

We had agreed to rendezvous in the imposing central park of Riga by the bronze statue of Lenin with his arms outstretched. It was a beautiful day as I arrived there. Children were playing delightedly on the well-manicured lawns that smelled fresh and verdant. I spotted Laura and ran towards her. She had flown in from Petrozavodsk and I had traveled on the night train from Tallinn. I hugged her tight in front of Lenin's stern gaze and, as agreed, she was accompanied by Pastor Joseph Bondarenko. Joseph held out his hand. His grip was firm and strong.

Joseph had the reputation of being "the Billy Graham of Russia." This slightly built man with dark, wavy hair, was an evangelist with fire in his bones. He was also the pastor of a 500-member congregation in Riga. In addition, I was aware that Joseph frequently organized evangelistic campaigns and youth rallies all over the former Soviet Union— something that was extremely risky to do.

Joseph's tolerant attitude toward other evangelical denominations in the USSR had caused discord among his brethren, not least the leader of the unregistered Baptists, Georgi Vins, who had been released from prison in an exchange under the Jimmy Carter administration. I had discovered that Laura had rejected an offer from Georgi to be his administrative assistant. This would have meant going underground, isolating herself from all contact with the outside world.

We strolled to the center of the park. We all talked openly about the problems Laura and I faced. "Joseph," she said in a deceptively soft voice, "I am not sure that marriage is God's will for my life. If I don't get a confirmation from the Lord, I know that our lives would be treacherous. In a worst case scenario, we would be bound by marriage, but we would be forbidden by earthly authorities to lead normal lives together."

In Joseph's presence, I then told of the "fleece" suggestion I had received in prayer.

"We could agree together before God," I suggested, "that if our marriage is in God's will, Laura should apply for a visa

75

to visit Finland. If she gets that visa, this would be the sign that we should get married."

"And what if she doesn't?" interjected Joseph, squinting in the bright sunlight.

"If she doesn't get the visa, then we will all know that it is not His will."

I looked at Laura and, without a moment's hesitation, she agreed. That was quick, I thought, and I soon found out why. She shared that she had already received two invitations to visit Finland. "Both times I applied, I was turned down for a visa," she said. "So it will definitely take a miracle for this to take place."

From a human standpoint, the situation looked impossible. "According to the authorities in Petrozavodsk, I am the wrong kind of person to represent the Soviet Union abroad," she revealed. "The Iron Curtain is airtight for people like me." In the 1970s, travel by Soviet citizens to the West was tightly regulated. Only a handful ever received visas.

As I heard this, I could not believe what I had just done. I had voluntarily suggested the impossible. The fleece did not have a chance!

An embarrassed look swept over my face. I took a deep breath and let it out slowly. In a state of panic, I said, "I withdraw my suggestion. This one doesn't have a chance." Laura was straining to hear my voice which was barely audible.

"No, it's a good fleece," said Laura. "Let it stand."

I was not aware that, before our meeting, Laura had consulted with Maria, Joseph's wife. Maria had asked Laura about Andrei, a gifted musician in Joseph's church, who had also proposed to her.

"I have prayed about it and I feel negatively about marrying Andrei," Laura had told her.

Laura then went on to say that there was an "even more interesting proposal from a Canadian believer." And then told Maria that I was younger by a few years.

She then asked Maria, "What do you think?"

To that, Maria said, "You still have time to say no. But never say no unless you have first prayed about it and have received a 'no' answer from the Lord."

Back at the park, Joseph stood thoughtfully for a moment, rubbing his forehead.

"Hannu," he finally said. "Do you love Laura?"

"Why yes," I replied.

"Laura, do you love Hannu," Joseph asked her.

After thinking it over for a brief moment, Laura said, "Yes."

"Well," he pressed on, "if you both love one another, then why the doubt? In my opinion, signs are not necessary. The matter should be pretty clear to both of you."

But Laura held fast to the "fleece" that I had suggested. She was not to be talked out of it, so Joseph closed our "open air" meeting in prayer.

"Lord," he said, "if it is Your Will for this couple to be married, please allow Laura to be granted a visa to visit Finland.

"If not, close the door right now."

Chapter Eleven

Romance In Danger

Winter had set in early and the snow was already knee-deep in Latvia on that day in November 1975, when I entered into the country accompanied by a group of believers from the West. The thick, white carpet that blanketed the countryside gave this Soviet republic a fairy tale appearance, affording us a picture-postcard view of the landscape out of the window of our train.

I had taken some time off from my photographic assignments for a further foray into the Soviet Union. On this occasion we were to enjoy the company of Veikko Manninen, the Secretary of Foreign Missions for the Pentecostal Movement of Finland, and an experienced world traveler who was constantly visiting Finnish missionaries at their outposts. Veikko had been into the Soviet Union on several occasions at the official invitation of the so-called Ministry of Religion of the USSR. In actual fact, the inviting party was the All Union Council of Evangelical Christians and Baptists of the USSR.

Our group also consisted of Ossi Valkama and Veikko Aijo, two Christians from the Finnish city of Nokia. They were heavy set men, both six feet tall and weighing in at about 220 pounds. Also in the party were Sirpa, Veikko Aijo's kid sister as well as two Norwegians: Per Oyvind Bastoye, who worked for a Christian ministry doing work in the USSR, and Hans Myrvold, who was spearheading a prayer program in the West for all of the Soviet Union.

Experience had taught that Riga would again be a tough place for Westerners to slip away from the watchful eye of the Intourist guides, who always kept tabs on their international guests.

Our main contact was to be Joseph Bondarenko who was under constant surveillance by the KGB, because of his many foreign contacts. They rightly suspected that this "warrior for Christ" was receiving a steady flow of literature and finances for the families of those evangelical ministers who were in prison for their faith. The KGB kept a round-the-clock observation on him in a bid to catch him in the act of receiving such sustenance.

Joseph was a constant thorn in the side of the KGB as he would travel around the USSR holding youth rallies, not large by western standards, but of unprecedented scale in his country.

After his conversion to Jesus Christ, Joseph had tasted the wrath of the Communist authorities. "Once, a newspaper came to interview me as a part of a broader article they were doing," commented Joseph. "They questioned me on my convictions and ministry."

When the feature was published, the following words appeared next to his interview: "People such as this are to be expelled from all universities and institutions of learning."

Bondarenko had been studying to be a shipbuilding engineer and was about to graduate. Shortly after the interview appeared, he was offered a bizarre choice: a job on the editorial staff of the same newspaper—or prison. Joseph had already dedicated his life and talents to God and went on to serve not just one, but several prison terms. But God was in prison with him and many inmates were won to the Lord in the camps he was incarcerated in.

"1957 was a time of real tribulation and isolation for us Christian young people," Bondarenko had said, "We started to pray that God would help us to establish contact with believers in the West, so that we might feel a unity in spirit and know that there were others who would help us carry our burden and pray for us. Our burden was truly heavy at that time.

"We also prayed for revival in our nation. In fasting and prayer, we received an assurance that there would be a special revival among the youth that would spread to the older folk as well. We decided to boldly proclaim Christ despite all of the consequences. We had to leave the results in God's hands.

"God, in his heaven, answered our prayers and we are happy for the fellowship. We were in a dark valley, but it is brighter now."

Bondarenko said that then, in 1975, there was revival in the churches among the youth.

As a group, we had gathered for a "Pow wow" before leaving. We discussed the itinerary, set by Joseph and his aides. We were to have talks in Joseph's home. Then, later that night, we were scheduled to take part in a "secret service" also to be held in Joseph's house.

Laura was to fly in from Petrozavodsk the day of our arrival and Vera, Laura's cousin, had already arrived and was waiting for our group outside the Hotel Riga. She nodded knowingly as we clambered out of the Intourist bus that had brought us from the station, but did not speak.

After putting our luggage in our rooms, we stepped outside to head out for our appointment with Joseph.

We were confronted in the lobby by Svetlana, a stunningly beautiful blonde Intourist guide. It was as if she had been present in our hotel room monitoring our every movement. "Where do you think you are all going?" she asked with deep suspicion registering in her gray-green eyes.

"In the direction of Yurmala," I answered for the rest of our contingent. I was aware that Yurmala was a popular spa-resort area frequented by tourists.

"That is good," she smiled.

I guessed she must be new to the job because she had mistakenly deduced that we were actually off to the resort.

"I think you should take the electric train," she suggested helpfully, obviously feeling that this could be a day off for her. "You won't be needing me then, will you?" she asked.

I smiled. I was relieved that we would not have an escort with us, at least for the day. Still, I began to feel an uneasiness in my spirit that I could not explain or shake off.

As we headed out into the streets of this beautiful city, with slush underfoot, Vera, Laura's cousin from Petrozavodsk, walked a few yards ahead of us to the main railway station. It just so happened, that Joseph's home was close to a station on the line to Yurmala and so it should not have seemed strange that we were on this train.

After getting on board and taking a seat opposite Valeri, Joseph Bondarenko's right-hand man who "just happened" to also be on the train, it began jerking forward and soon the sights of Riga were flying past the window.

From my angle in the carriage, I could conveniently see the doorway leading into the coach we were in. Everyone was already expressionless, so it was odd that my eyes should fix on anyone special. But they did. There was a tall young man sitting near the door. The fact that he would occasionally glance in my direction, perked up my senses.

After twenty-minutes of eye-to-eye dueling with this young man, the train slowed down.

"We are nearly there," whispered Valeri. "We need to get off at the next stop."

At the Ogre station, which was halfway to Yurmala, we gingerly stepped down onto the snow-covered platform. It was so deep that we sank down halfway to our knees.

With Valeri in the lead, we started the slippery hike to our destination. I thought with great joy that we would soon be in Joseph's company. That was presumptuous. Our itinerary was about to change abruptly. After we had walked scarcely a hundred yards from the station, two black Volga cars slid to a halt in the road beside us. The doors swung open and four men from each car, all but one of them in militia uniforms and furashkas (pilot-style hats) jumped out. The plainclothes man seemed to be in charge and he ordered the others to surround us as if we were escaped convicts. Even if we had wanted to, there was no way we could try to make a run for it in such slippery conditions.

"Stop! You're under arrest," bellowed the man without a uniform in Russian.

"Documents! Passports!" roared one of the militiamen.

Valeri and Vera dug out their internal passports and handed them over. Of course, those of us from the West, did not have ours. It was common practice in the Soviet Union at that time for Intourist to take all international passports into their "safekeeping" the moment a foreigner arrived at his or her destination.

"You already know that our friends do not have their passports with them," said Vera, as we stood there, a ring of men around us.

Even as she spoke, a black police van pulled in behind us. The men then began roughly grabbing us and herding us into the filthy vehicle.

As the door was slammed shut and we were driven away, each of us sitting on a soiled bench seat along the side of the enclosed rear cabin, I felt my emotions, which had become as taut as a bow string on a violin, about to snap. As we bumped along, an appalling thought struck me. Was this the end of my romance with Laura? I was all too aware of the consequences of this piece of drama. The KGB, in Riga, had been waiting for this very opportunity.

In the ruckus, I suddenly noticed that I was seated next to Vera. Spontaneously I started to assemble a farewell speech to Laura. Vera would be my courier.

"Vera," I began, a large lump appearing in my throat, "it looks like this is the end of the road. I'll never see Laura again. Please tell her that I love her and that I will never forget her as long as I live."

A surprised smile crept into Vera's face. Perhaps, I surmised, she had never been too happy about our possible marriage in the first place. Vera was single and Laura, to her, was like an only child. Still, she promised to relay my message to Laura.

After a few minutes, the police vehicle's brakes squealed as it came to a stop outside the Ogre police station, an unpretentious wooden building. We were shepherded into a large room furnished sparingly with one table and half a dozen wooden chairs.

I choked back my surprise, when the door opened and there stood the same young man I had spotted on the train. His smirk revealed that he was satisfied with his mission.

Momentarily, the police chief, a heavily built man dressed in a well-tailored gray uniform of jacket and pants, entered the room. Before delivering a short speech pointing out that we had "broken Soviet law governing the movement of foreigners inside the country," he took off his hat and laid it on the table in front of him, revealing a thick shade of black hair with some thin strands of gray.

It was not long before Valeri was taken away for interrogation. He never returned and we discovered later that he had been released after a night-long grilling.

After Valeri had left, the police chief walked over to me, handed me a pen and, through Vera who was acting as the unofficial interpreter, told me to sign the blank piece of paper.

"Is he kidding?" I asked Vera. I had heard enough stories about people being sent to Siberian labor camps after making such a stupid mistake.

"Please tell the chief that I cannot sign this piece of paper unless a Canadian consular officer is present," I instructed Vera.

The man stood towering above me, his temper by now burning on a short fuse. With one hand he grabbed my right wrist and with the other he picked up the pen he had just laid on the table and jabbed it into my fist. Then he slammed my hand against the blank white paper and yelled, "Peeshee!" which, in Russian, means "Write!"

As soon as he loosened his grip, I defiantly cast the pen so that it bounced along the table and onto the floor. He stormed out of the room shouting words in Russian that I did not understand, nor wished to.

It was now Vera's turn to be questioned. She was led away by one of the militiamen. She did not return into our company.

The lone police officer in the room with us then told us that we would be transported back to our hotel where staff from Intourist would continue the interrogation.

The militiamen drove us to the Hotel Riga and then frog-marched us into the Intourist director's second floor office. I guessed the director, a woman, to be in her mid-to-late forties. She was slim and attractive with brown hair. The director began by rebuking us for "unlawfully" leaving the city limits.

"You had no right to travel to Ogre," she railed. "It is out of bounds for tourists."

Deportation was now a virtual certainty. For my Western colleagues, it was a sad situation, but for me it was a disaster. For Laura lived in the Soviet Union.

There was only one thread of hope left and that was the guide that we had talked to in the morning. I explained to the director that we did not know we had broken any law.

"One of your guides gave us permission to go without her company," I pointed out.

The director obviously did not believe me. "That's a fabrication," she screamed. "Nobody would give you such permission!" she added angrily.

"I can prove it," I said, standing my ground.

"What is the name of the guide who gave you this permission?" she asked.

"I don't know her name, but if you call in all of your guides, I can point her out to you."

The director thought it over for a moment then she responded. "You can go to your rooms," she said. "Come back here in an hour."

We reassembled in her office at the appointed time. All seven of the female guides were there and all were young ladies. I felt sick to my stomach for I was well aware what this meant for one of them.

The director called for silence and then, turning to me abruptly, she asked, "Who was the one who told you that you could leave the city without a guide?"

I drew a deep breath. It was obvious that my words would devastate Svetlana, whose face had by now drained of all color. I knew she would be fired as a consequence of my revelation and I wanted to disappear. I had to balance, however, my actions with the fact that my deportation and exile could mean the unthinkable—separation forever from Laura.

I mustered all my courage and slowly lifted my right hand and pointed to Svetlana. It was if I had shot her with a handgun. She immediately began to cry and covered her face with her hands.

The director did not seem to be impressed with what she considered to be Svetlana's histrionics.

"You are requested to go to your rooms," she ordered us. "You will be notified about our decision. You may have to leave for Leningrad tonight."

Veikko Manninen, being a man of principle, interjected, "We are not leaving this room until you promise us that we can remain in Riga according to our original itinerary. We will leave tomorrow, and no sooner." His facial expressions reminded me of a few Soviet border guards that I had seen.

The director finally relented. I was relieved, but I knew that even though we had won this battle, I could not be sure that I would be given the opportunity to ever return to the Soviet Union.

On the next occasion I applied for a visa, I would find out!

Underground service in Petrozavodsk at the height of persecution.

Laura at a baptismal service in her home church.

Chapter Twelve

Check Point
"Club Country"

Checkpoint "Club Country" loomed ominously through the floating tendrils of mist as our Volkswagen Kleinbus drove the last few yards from the moonscape terrain of Finland into Russia. Once again, the by now familiar nervous anticipation overtook me as I saw the high watchtowers in the sky.

Our multi-national group wanted to test out this border crossing that had opened up just a few months prior to our trip.

"Checkpoint Charlie" and "Checkpoint Bravo," were great sounding crossing points into East Germany. Something more bizarre was the fact that the Finns named the Soviet frontier post, "Checkpoint Club Country," after the famed wooden club carried by the pre-historic cave dwellers of the area. These uniformed Soviet guards, however, did not carry clubs, but automatic weapons.

As my heartbeat began to pick up with nervous anticipation, we pulled up beside the small pavilion that housed the

Russian frontier personnel. It was a small building, but it carried an atmosphere that was, to me, very threatening.

I had to admit to being surprised when I was again granted a visa to visit the Soviet Union. With much prayer, I had completed the form and handed it to the travel agency, and was pleased when they called a few days later.

"Hannu," she said, knowing of my previous trip, "you're in. They've granted you the necessary travel document."

Laura was scheduled to visit Finland in March if all went well, but it was still February and I decided to make another trip into Russia to see Laura. I joined a group of Christians that consisted of seven people: the driver, Timo Tormas, from Finland; Rob, a Swiss believer; Satish, from India; Juhani Nordblom, a missionary from Thailand; and three Canadian Finns: Aki, Jyrki and myself.

We were aware that the bulk of traffic still flowed from Finland through the other checkpoints of Vainikkala and Vaalimaa and so we hoped that the "Club Country" crossing would be operated by less vigilant guards and so we would not be subjected to the usual intensive scrutiny.

All was quiet when our van pulled up in front of the pavilion. My heart dropped when I saw that ours was the only vehicle at customs. I surmised that the cold weather had kept potential eastbound tourists at home. I did not like the look of things. We were sitting ducks for the officers as they had no one else to take care of. I was "clean." I had no Bibles in my possession. It was a precaution that I had taken knowing that any incident at the border could close the doors on me.

The customs agent, wearing a smart newly pressed pale green uniform, with a light green shirt and matching tie, walked over to us.

"Passports and visas," he said curtly. Tim, our driver, gathered them from us and handed them to the guard through the window. With that, he disappeared into the building, while another officer stepped forward and ordered us to unload our luggage and take it inside.

I breathed a sigh of relief when, after a quick check of my bags, nothing untoward was found. But then I spotted another officer who had been standing off to the side, carefully paying attention to all of us.

His eyes had been fixed on Satish, who had become tired of waiting. Sitting down in one corner of the customs hall, our Indian friend crossed and uncrossed his legs anxiously, bowed his head toward the floor, and then balanced himself standing on his head and hands. I could not believe what I was seeing. Whether Satish intended to or not, his gyrations had drawn attention to himself and sparked the officer's suspicion.

I felt like screaming out to him to stop doing this; that at Soviet customs, people generally stand quietly in line and behaved in a normal fashion.

The officer left his position and shouted out that he wanted a "spot body check" on some of us.

"You," he said, pointing a finger at Juhani, "follow me."

As I watched my Thai friend leave for a room down the corridor, I got panicky. However, my fear proved unfounded. Juhani quickly returned, a nervous smile covering his face.

"Don't worry," he whispered. "They found nothing."

The officer then requested Aki to follow him. I held my breath again because I knew he had literature concealed on him. Time passed agonizingly slowly and Aki had still not reappeared. I shot up a prayer to heaven that he would be safe.

Inside the side room, the soldier moved his hand along Aki's back, chest, sleeves and trousers. He suddenly felt two bumps on Aki's waist and, with a shout of triumph, pulled out two Russian Bibles that had been taped to Aki's stomach.

"Why did you bring these books into our country?" he screamed, his face twisting down in anger. "They are not needed here!"

The agent spoke poor Finnish and Aki could not speak Russian. Lacking a common language, Aki took one of the Bibles from a table where they had been thrown and opened it up to John, Chapter 3, verse 16. He held the open Bible in the direction of the agent, pointing to the verse.

The inspecting officer began reading out loud, "For God so loved the world that He gave His only begotten Son, that whosoever believeth in Him... " He stopped short.

Without warning, the interrogator ripped the Bible from Aki's hand and, in a fit of rage, tossed it into a corner of the small room. With a splat, the black Bible hit the floor in an untidy heap, its pages flapping open.

"There is no God," he yelled as the veins in his neck rose up like strands of spaghetti. "This book is a pack of fables! All of it."

I knew something was wrong, when this man appeared out of the back office.

"Dosmotrim vse!" he shouted through blanched lips, meaning, "We will check them all."

Aki and Jyrki were both members of the church in Vancouver, that was also my home church. Like me, they were children of parents who had left Finland and moved to North America. We had even attended the same young people's meetings and youth camps, although the pair were several years my junior.

While visiting Finland, Aki and Jyrki had decided to visit the Soviet Union for the first time. They had asked me to get them some Russian Bibles as gifts for local believers. I had consented, but sternly warned that I could not be associated with the books—especially if something went wrong at customs. It was important for me to be able to travel to see Laura. I had made it clear to them that if they were caught, under no circumstances, were they to reveal where they got the books.

"Should a problem arise, your are on your own," I told them.

The two had agreed that my future with Laura would not be jeopardized.

I stood petrified near the entrance to the hallway where Aki was undergoing his ordeal. After what seemed like an eternity, Aki reappeared. His face was pale.

"Did they find the books?" I whispered as he walked by. He nodded and I did not dare to ask any more.

Jyrki was next. Time was now my greatest tormentor, as minute beads of perspiration sprung up on my forehead. I could not bear the agony of waiting. I was well aware that these two boyhood friends were ill-equipped to withstand the psychological strain they would encounter at Soviet customs.

The minutes continued to tick by ever so slowly. Finally, Jyrki came through the door like a puppy with his tail between his legs. He walked by me, and spoke some words that had a paralyzing effect on me.

"Hannu, I confessed everything," he said, showing a sudden spasm of remorse. "I told them that I got the literature from you!" His voice shook and his face turned pale.

I groaned as my fears mounted. I tried to swallow, but found that I could not. A dragging sense of bewildered desolation began to overwhelm me.

Then I heard my name being called by the officer who was having a field day. In total confusion, I marched after him to the search room. I knew what to expect. At his suggestion, I took my seat on one of the two chairs in the otherwise bare room. The official sat down opposite me. He did not seem angry. But I knew that was a cover for his real emotions.

"Do you have any literature with you," he asked with feigned friendliness.

"No," I stated as calmly as physically possible.

"Please stand up," he went on. "I will have to see for myself if you are telling the truth."

His fingers skillfully checked me over and all he found were two Christian music cassettes. Without showing a flicker of animosity, he said, "Mr. Haukka, you are very well informed about Soviet customs regulations. That is why you did not bring anything with you personally, except for these two cassettes. But it is a greater crime to provoke others to break the law and try and bring in banned literature."

The officer was not asking a question, rather making a statement. At that point, he made it clear that the interview was over and he ordered me to return to the main hall.

Every one in our party had now been searched and literature had been discovered on four in the group. Before we had left Finland, I had not bothered asking my colleagues who had books and who did not.

The drama was not over yet. Another officer proceeded to pull Timo and myself to one side.

"Is there any literature in the car?" he asked.

"Not to my knowledge," replied a visibly perplexed Timo who tried to sound normal, but his voice was too high.

"Good," said the officer, adding, "so if I find even one page of a Bible or any other religious book in your vehicle, we will confiscate it. You have one last chance to retrieve any hidden literature. If you act voluntarily, nothing will happen to the vehicle. Think about it one more time. Are there any books in the car?" he asked.

"None," replied Timo.

Even as he spoke, a terrible thought struck me. I remembered that I had stuffed two large-size Russian Bibles into a sleeping bag and that bag was still in the automobile.

I frantically looked for a way to warn Timo. At that moment, he was whisked outside to the van.

What could I do? The customs agents swarmed into the vehicle that belonged to a local church in Helsinki. Timo, who worked at the church, the largest Evangelical church in Finland, had borrowed it for the trip under the condition that it would be safely returned, preferably undamaged.

I watched through a window as the vehicle was driven up on props and a special customs squad got to work on it. They tore at upholstery, unscrewed sections, poked, and searched every conceivable space, nook, cranny, chamber, padding and seam..

About an hour passed as the men worked in the unyieldingly cold temperature outside. Finally, Timo and his hosts stepped inside the heated hall. Timo was shivering, not only from the arctic cold, but also from the ordeal. I searched his facial expressions to try to detect what had happened outside. Maybe a sign of grief would reveal the conclusion, but there was no emotion in his face.

We had, by now, been at Checkpoint "Club Country" for six hours. The officials disappeared to a side room for consultations. Mentally, I had prepared myself for my expulsion from the country to Finland. Again, I constructed a last farewell for Laura.

The men returned and shoulder to shoulder took up positions in front of us.

The senior officer then handed Timo and Juhani their passports.

"You are welcome to continue your trip," he told them.

The commanding officer then turned his attention to Rob and Satish.

"This is your first time in our country," he said. "In your ignorance, you have broken our laws. Still, you may continue your trip. But," he warned, "if you ever decide to come back, please take our laws into consideration. You will not get off so lightly on the next occasion."

Surprisingly, Aki and Jyrki were also given their passports back. The officer told them that they were "still young and it was desirable for them to get a proper picture of the Soviet Union."

He paused and then added, "However, should your offense ever be repeated, you will be in deep trouble." the man stopped to allow the significance of his words to sink in.

Now came my turn and I steeled myself for his verdict. "But you," he scolded, as I shivered, feeling as if the very ground under my feet was no longer solid, "...you are the real culprit. You are the root cause of this," he said with tired irritation. "You supplied the others with the literature. There is no justification for us to allow you to continue your journey under any circumstances. You should be turned back!"

I was now sobbing on the inside as the dread shadow of instant expulsion loomed over me. So, I was not prepared for the next part of his diatribe.

"We really don't know why, but we have decided to allow you to continue your travel—for the last time," he said, glowering at me—as his voice building into a crescendo.

"But, let me make it clear that if we ever discover even a small transgression by yourself, you can be sure that you will never again be allowed into our country.

"Do you understand?"

Incredible, I thought. God this has to be you. Then thinking of the verses in Psalm 91 I whispered to Him, "You have sheltered me with Your wings."

I nodded, sighing deeply with relief. Silently, I thanked the Lord for softening the hearts of these Communist officers. God was sovereign. He had controlled the circumstances. He had intervened in an impossible situation that I had written off.

We stumbled out of the main entrance of the customs pavilion in a daze, taking our baggage, minus the Bibles and music cassettes, with us.

Timo turned on the ignition and the VW engine sprang to life.

A couple of hundred yards down the road, everyone burst into spontaneous praise to the Lord for the great thing He had done. Just then, I remembered something. I reached for the sleeping bag still on the floor of the van, pulled on the strings that secured it, and out tumbled two large Bibles.

"Where was this thing during the inspection?" I asked Timo. I saw bewilderment sweep his face.

"Well, first it was on the front seat, then on the floor, then on the back seat, then outside in the snow," he replied. "They just tossed it around from place to place," he added, grinning widely.

"That's amazing, simply amazing!" I repeated aloud and sighed again.

Only a few hours remained to the departure of the train we needed to connect with at Leningrad railway station. And we were still in Viborg. Under the treacherous conditions of an early winter, high speed on Soviet highways was extremely dangerous. Still, we had to make the train, so Timo stepped on the gas and the van sped onwards, leaving behind us swirls of snow.

Chapter Thirteen

An Appointment With Faith

An ancient Russian bus waddled through the bleak streets of Petrozavodsk carrying Laura to her appointment with faith. The twenty-minute journey to the passport office seemed to last an eternity for her. She sat next to a babushka clad in a heavy gray overcoat and wearing a weary expression revealing that life had become too much for her to bear.

As Laura was heading towards the big interview, the elderly lady was riding downtown to stand in line for four hours to get one precious loaf of bread.

The bus came to a grinding halt with an ear-piercing squeal from the brakes and Laura got up from her seat and exited the bus at the back.

At that time in the Soviet Union, there were three institutions in whose hands the reigns of power rested: the Soviet military, the KGB, and the Ministry of Internal Affairs. All three were closely connected and were much feared by the ordinary people.

Laura stepped nervously through the doorway of the Visa and Registration Section of the Ministry of Internal Affairs. She had long waited for her summons to visit the KGB headquarters for the problems she had encountered in Riga, but none had come. Obviously, our romance would have been over if she had been prosecuted.

After that fateful arrest, she had been put on the train to Murmansk, which stopped briefly at Petrozavodsk. She expected to be met by the police as she stepped off the train, but there was no one there so she had headed home to be tearfully reunited with her mother. Laura was free to move around her city, but everything is relative. There was no place to hide. The country, let alone her home city, was one big prison camp. Laura was aware that she could be summoned at any moment by the KGB—when it was convenient for them.

But unexplainably, the summons never came, so she decided to try to get a visa to visit Finland.

Laura had carefully filled out her application form. She had enclosed various references including the all-important employer's statement of conduct. After being rejected on her two previous attempts to travel to Finland, Laura had little faith that she would be granted the necessary travel documents and be given a passport.

However, the fleece had been agreed on and she would test it out. Laura was resolute in her decision. If God was interested in her future and her marriage to a Canadian, then He would perform a miracle. Only then would Laura believe that it was clear that God was behind the proposed marriage and would bless it.

At the reception desk, a serious-looking woman looked up at her and then took the papers, scanning the employer's statement through her heavy eyeglasses. Laura knew that this typewritten disclosure had the power to kill any faint hope she had to make the trip. The woman stopped reading, looked up at Laura's pale features and said, "You don't really expect to go anywhere with this kind of document."

She read out loud the words, ". . . executes her duties well, but is politically untrustworthy. Does not take part in social activity (meaning the Communist party), and is not to be recommended for travel abroad."

Laura's face was drawn and tense but her response to the receptionist's query was frank. "I will not ask for another reference," she said in a soft but determined voice, "because I know that another one will not be issued to me. Please accept these papers just as they are."

The receptionist looked at Laura with a hint of pity in her eyes. "If you say so, but take it from me that you do not have the slightest chance of being granted the necessary papers."

* * * * *

Laura's fingers trembled as she tore open the envelope that bore the words, Ministry of Internal Affairs printed in big bold letters in the left hand corner.

Her emotions were just below the surface like a volcano, ready to erupt.

Laura squinted in the darkness of the living room of her home as she read to herself, "You are hereby summoned to this office concerning your application to travel to Finland." Laura knew that the moment of truth was at hand. What would they say?

The same receptionist was on duty. As she saw Laura standing before her, she shook her head in astonishment. The woman reached out on her desk to find Laura's papers and handed them to her, still shaking her head.

"It has never happened before," she stated. "I cannot figure out how you have been granted permission. It doesn't make any sense."

Laura was stunned and happy at the same time. A joyful smile covered her face. It made all the sense in the world to her. It was truly God's sign! God had responded to her fleece, like Gideon's long ago.

* * * * *

Laura had to wait a whole day in Leningrad to catch the train to Helsinki. There was no direct connection to Helsinki from Petrozavodsk. We had agreed that Laura would be at a friend's home who had a telephone. I would call her that day at a given time.

Her voice was strangely hushed and nervous as she told me that she would be at the railroad station in Helsinki the next morning. But the Iron Curtain was still up and she was on the other side. Nothing was certain until the train had crossed through the Soviet-Finnish frontier onto Finnish soil. The Soviet border guards had the right to pull anyone off the train at any time without offering an explanation. Their system provided for such conduct. It was totally possible that the authorities had been just teasing Laura by letting her think that she was going somewhere when, in actual fact, she would be ambushed at the border.

It was a dull day at the Central Railway Station in Helsinki. The sky was overcast and the platform was slushy. Even though it was now March 1976, a winter snow struggled to hold its ground in the face of the approaching spring.

Ten Christian friends joined me outside the terminal building to see whether Laura would really be on the incoming train from Leningrad. Every one of them knew Laura personally. They had fellowshiped, prayed, and rejoiced together with her in Petrozavodsk. A number of the group had been blacklisted and were banned from the Soviet Union because of their activities. They had not seen Laura for a long time.

I, like my friends, thought we would not be seeing her. We were people of little faith, but we still had enough to be there—just in case of a miracle.

One of those standing by me voiced her doubts. "I won't believe it until I see her," she said.

This was not an overstatement.

Even Laura, up until the last moment, expected to hear the words, "We have changed our minds. You are not leaving after all."

The suspense mounted by the second as the green-colored coaches of Soviet Railways churned to a stop outside the Helsinki terminal. Momentarily, passengers began disembarking. There were several Soviet coaches, so it was not easy to spot our arriving party.

Suddenly, I saw the lovely figure of Laura. She was wearing a long, violet winter coat, black knee-high leather boots and a knitted dark-brown wool hat with a light trim. On the platform, about thirty yards away, she began dragging her big vinyl suitcase and hand-luggage towards us. The spirit of "Doubting Thomas" had us captive, and we stood as if riveted to the ground as if we had seen a ghost. In her excitement, Laura began to walk faster, breathlessly heaving her luggage towards us.

Finally, I awoke and tried to take charge of the situation. The others joined and ran in her direction, picking up her bags, hugging her and laughing and crying all at the same time.

I took Laura in my shaking arms and we wept together. With our eyes damp with joy, she looked at me. The sign had come to pass and God had spoken. I was relieved, thankful and happy, all at the same time.

"Welcome Laura," was all I could say.

God had spoken and we now had to obey. After Laura had enjoyed her first sleep in the West, we decided to go and visit a jeweler in the city. I watched Laura's eyes light up with delight as we wandered hand-in-hand through the streets of Helsinki and gazed into store windows. What was normal for me, was extraordinary for her.

"I have never seen so many goods for sale," she chuckled in amazement. "And there are no lines for food."

"Laura," I said, squeezing her hand, "things are different here."

She shook her head in disbelief. After a few minutes, we reached the jeweler where she was to pick out the engagement ring. The clerk behind the counter could not have been more helpful. He brought out tray after tray of sparkling diamond rings for her to look over.

Finally, she settled on a lovely ring with a lone diamond in it. "That's the one I want," she declared. "Can I try it on?"

Before she could do just that, I took it from the clerk and lovingly placed it on the third finger of her left hand.

"There we are," I said, hardly able to contain my joy. "Now we are officially engaged!"

Her eyes were as big as saucers as she gazed down at the ring, reflecting light into her face from the street outside.

"Hannu, it's quite lovely," she exclaimed. "I thought I would never own such a ring."

We embraced and I asked the clerk if she could leave it on.

"My wife-to-be is from Russia," I explained.

"Oh, congratulations," was his response. "I know you will both be very happy."

We were engaged in Helsinki on March 7. The engagement party was held in the home of Mary Yrjölä, who had known Laura since the late sixties. Mary had been exiled from Russia for bringing in printed Christian material for the children's ministry of Laura's church.

It was a joyful affair. Most of those who attended the celebration had been blacklisted from reentering the Soviet Union. All of them had met Laura in Russia. They were fully aware of her story and, like myself, were astonished that she was finally in Finland.

During the three weeks that Laura was in Helsinki, we were inseparable.

"We need to set a date for the wedding," I told Laura one day.

"You mean our weddings!" she countered.

I was puzzled by what she meant by "weddings!"

"Hannu," she explained, "we first have to go through a civil ceremony before we can have the church wedding."

"Where then should we get married?" I asked.

"Riga," she said firmly.

After more discussion, we settled on July as the month we would officially link our lives together. That was just three months away, so I knew my work would be cut out to get the right papers issued.

Laura explained to me that weddings performed out of the country involving Soviet citizens, were not recognized by the Soviets. In order for me to be married in the Soviet Union, the authorities there required legal papers that were not available in Canada. And, because international marriages of this kind were rare in the 1970s and international marriages between Christians were unheard of, there were really no precedents.

It was now time for Laura to board the train back to Russia. I accompanied her to the railway station with mixed feelings. One part of me had hoped she would somehow stay on in the West, but Laura had promised the authorities that she would only stay for three weeks, and she was determined to stick to her word.

I carried her luggage to the train and, before she boarded it, we embraced again and I told her once again that I loved her.

"I love you, too, Hannu," she said softly. "It won't be much longer before we can be together forever."

With that, Laura picked up her bags and climbed aboard the train.

I watched with sadness as the train began pulling out of the station. I waved to Laura and she waved back through the window. Soon, she had disappeared and was on her way back to Russia. I now had to get to work to make sure all was in place for me to travel to Riga for the ceremonies.

* * * * *

" Hey, Hannu," said one of my friends at the publishing house, "I had an interesting visit today from a guy from SUPO [the Finnish Intelligence Agency]. The man wanted to know why you had returned to Finland from Canada and what your political affiliations were."

I was dumfounded.

"They were carrying out an investigation on your background and they're asking all those who possibly know you. I guess they want to discover why you want to marry a girl from Russia."

My friend revealed that the intelligence officer had warned him not to tell me about the investigation, but he thought I should know what was happening.

In May I returned to Vancouver to start the task of compiling the documentation necessary for the registration of our marriage in Russia. I also wanted it to be legal in Canada.

Not only were the KGB in Russia and State Security in Finland, interested in my plans, now my upcoming marriage was stirring interest with Canadian Intelligence. I had only been home for twenty-four hours, when I discovered that Canada has a secret service. The phone rang in my home. It was a friend of the family from the RCMP (Royal Canadian Mounted Police).

"I think we should meet," he said down the line.

"What for?" I asked bemused.

"Your twenty or so trips to the Soviet Union," he replied.

I could not believe what I was hearing. How did he know about my visits there?

* * * * *

I answered the ring of our front door bell. As I opened the door, I was confronted by two burly plainclothes officers who, according to their ID, were from counter intelligence.

"Mr. Haukka," said one of them. "Can we come in? We have some important matters to discuss with you."

After lengthy questioning, one of the officers finally came to the point. "Mr. Haukka, we need to know if you have been the subject of any pressure or possible blackmail during your visits to the Soviet Union."

I rubbed my chin and then told them of the various problems I had encountered at the border and also within the country. They listened with keen interest as I recounted some of my experiences.

"Tell us about Laura," the man then asked.

I told them about Laura's remarkable testimony. How she had found God in Russia, her expulsion from university and her most recent arrest in Riga.

"We just want to tell you Hannu, that we are here to help you in case the Soviet authorities present a problem for Laura," he said. "If this should happen, we will be right there to help you in any way we can."

I expressed my thanks to the men, but I had my doubts as to what exactly they could do. If God was not on our side, I was convinced that no earthly authority could "twist the arm" of the Soviet authorities.

The Canadian marriage law did not require a certificate proving a person was single. The difference was a technicality. Canadian government records could verify that there was no marriage registered under the name of Hannu Haukka in Canada, for example. I was free to get married, but the wording did not actually state that Hannu Haukka was not married. Unfortunately, wording was important to the Soviets.

The solution was found through Ari Anas, a Finnish-Canadian lawyer. He set to work to write up a document to satisfy the Soviet authorities that then had to be endorsed by the Ministry of Health in the Province of British Columbia. Endorsement was also needed from the Soviet Embassy in Ottawa.

I was told that in order for Laura to receive an exit permit, a letter of invitation had to be addressed to the director of the visa department of the Karelian Autonomous Soviet Republic—a province of Russia. In this letter, I had to guarantee that I would assume total financial responsibility for my wife's well-being after her exit. This paper was to be endorsed by the Ministry of Internal Affairs in Finland and the Soviet Embassy in Helsinki.

It was not long before potential storm clouds appeared on the horizon. Surprisingly, the Soviet Embassy in Ottawa was hanging on to the Canadian documentation that needed endorsing.

The days ticked by and in desperation I departed for Finland empty-handed. All attempts by my Canadian lawyer to retrieve the critical papers proved futile. The Soviet Embassy in the Canadian Capitol would not release the papers. By now they had been in Ottawa for over six weeks for a bureaucratic procedure that should have taken no more than fifteen minutes.

Each time my attorney called them, he was told, "The documents are still being processed." I knew this was the Soviets' way of saying, "We do not approve of this marriage."

The dates for our "ceremonies" were drawing closer with each passing day. I made up my mind that I could not wait any longer. With a steel-like sense of purpose I decided that I would be leaving for Russia in a few days.

As a last resort, I told my lawyer to take the papers personally to any aircraft bound for Helsinki, should the Embassy finally "wake up." I would be at the airport to pick them up.

They never came!

I prayed a last desperate prayer for God's intervention. It was my appointment with faith!

Chapter Fourteen

Trouble And Tranquility

I stood transfixed before the huge hammer and sickle on the wall of the Marriage Palace of Petrozavodsk, a government registration office for marriages. Laura was wearing a red jumper and a white blouse as she stood at my side. Directly in front of us was a well-groomed woman attorney of hefty proportions and indeterminate late middle age. She wore a blue and red ribbon draped diagonally around her shoulder and waist.

The long-awaited day had arrived—Friday, July 23, 1976.

The actual church ceremony, common only to believers, was scheduled to take place two days later on Sunday, in a local church affiliated with the Union of Evangelical Christians and Baptists, a coalition of Pentecostals and Baptists.

The state wedding really should never have taken place as none of the required papers were with me. They were still under lock and key at the Soviet Embassy in Ottawa. The only legal document I had with me was my Canadian passport. Both Laura and I suspected that the KGB had intervened, possibly to demonstrate a kind side of the "Big Bad Bear" of Russia, by issuing an order to execute the wedding registration without incident. Why it had been issued was a mystery—unless, of course, as we saw it, there had been intervention from a yet Higher Authority!

The Petrozavodsk KGB was obviously set to allow the event to take place and they even allowed five Canadians to accompany me: my brother, John, as well as Dr. and Mrs. Kaarlo Suomela, friends of both our families, and Mr. and Mrs. Larry Kokkonen. My parents did not attend the wedding, probably out of fear of the Soviet Union. My grandfather on my mother's side was killed by the Russians during the Second World War leaving six infants behind. My own father, like most Finns, had bad memories of Russia.

After the short ceremony in which the attorney declared us "man and wife," she asked us to exchange wedding bands. Then she launched into a monologue in Russian, translated for me by Laura, which wished our marriage permanence and faithfulness.

"I would like to counsel you both to establish a good, harmonious Soviet family that will grow up in the spirit of communism and become worthy citizens," she added in a no-nonsense voice as I shuffled uncomfortably as Laura and I both stood together, holding each other's hand as she whispered to me what was being said.

After the to-the-point speech, I leaned across to Laura and planted a kiss on her lips, then gazed at her with my heart in my eyes.

Although we were now legally man and wife, we did not consider we were actually married in the sight of God until the church ceremony. So, after the state wedding, I went to my hotel to sleep that night and Laura went to her home.

Originally, we had planned that we would take the train to Riga the next day where the ceremony was to take place in Joseph Bondarenko's church in front of Laura's many friends and seventy international guests. Joseph, true to his great administrative skills, had been busy organizing a grand celebration. It was to be a historic wedding where East met West—in more ways than one.

There was a potential stumbling block. The wedding could not take place without the knowledge of the authorities. The endeavor was in troubled waters from the beginning. Oddly enough, not one single vacant hotel room could be found in Riga. Western travel agencies could not file a tourist visa application without confirmed booking for hotel rooms. That was the way state security controlled and monitored the flow of tourists and their movements within the country.

This meant, bluntly, that I could not attend my own wedding, unless I had a hotel booking, and I did not have one.

On a previous trip to Riga, Laura had been summoned to the KGB headquarters. Edward, an officer who was in charge of the little known Fifth Division (the arm of the KGB responsible for religious affairs) welcomed Laura into his office.

"So you are planning on having a wedding," he said.

She nodded, so he got straight to the point.

"If you can talk Pastor Bondarenko into registering his church, then we will allow you to have your wedding in this city. If not, I'm sorry. It won't fly."

The KGB had long tried to force Bondarenko to register his group, thus effectively placing it under KGB supervision. The pastor was aware that each church that registered was obliged to submit a full list of the names and addresses of its adherents. Pastors were regularly subject to discipline, rebuke and open threats by the KGB whenever church activity began to appear too evangelistic or successful.

Regulation was tough. When a church was registered, the pastor was forced to sign a document that prohibited him from a whole assortment of "harmful" activities. Among them was that he was not permitted to have a children's ministry, no Sunday school, no attendance of young people under the age of eighteen, no youth meetings, no youth choirs and a minimum age of baptisms of eighteen years. In addition, there was to be no international or domestic speaker without prior clearance by the KGB. It was no wonder that many Soviet pastors could not accept these conditions. The moral compromise for them was too great.

To persuade Pastor Bondarenko was something that Laura would never agree to do.

"Excuse me," she said, "but who am I to advise Joseph as to what to do with his church?"

Edward's face turned red in ill-disguised anger. "Fine," he hissed, "your case is closed."

Our plans to get married in Riga had just slammed into a brick wall at the end of a dead-end street. The situation appeared to be desperate. The wedding would not take place. To add to the drama was the fact that no reception halls or restaurants were available to us in Riga.

The wedding had to be switched to the Baptist Church of Petrozavodsk. This was an All Union Council Church that Laura's unregistered group frequently attended.

* * * * *

It was now 10:00 AM and I was wearing a black suit with a white shirt and bow tie and my best man, Valeri Zakevich, Joseph Bondarenko's right-hand man stood at my side.

It was a magnificent sunny morning with hardly a cloud in the sky as Laura of Russia and Hannu of Canada were about to link lives together.

Valeri had picked me up in a Lada at the Hotel Pohjola where I was staying and then we drove to Laura's home where she joined us in the car. As we made our way to the church, I recalled the first time I had seen Laura. Her snow-white beauty had caused my heart to miss a few beats, and the same was happening now. She was spellbindingly beautiful. Her hair was done up in a special way that made her even more attractive. She was wearing a full-length white wedding gown from Finland with a veil down to her hips that was stunning.

Her hair was done up in a special way that made her even more attractive.

It was amazing that Laura looked so lovely. The night before the wedding, she had been up until four in the morning, taking care of accommodations for many of the 200 guests who had arrived from Moscow, Leningrad, Kiev, and many other cities. She had been dealing with visitors who had turned up at her home, holding her address in their hands. This was not unusual in the Soviet Union. You had to be prepared for anything as communications were so bad.

I was beaming with joy as she sat down beside me in the car. I must have stared at Laura with love in my eyes all the way to the church, because I do not recall seeing anything but her.

The road leading to the sanctuary was not paved and was full of potholes and tested the car's primitive suspension to the limit.

When we arrived at the church, we got out of the car and walked up the plank walkway from the road to the wooden steps into the sanctuary, where Joseph Bondarenko and Kai Antturi, pastor of a three-thousand member church in Helsinki, awaited us to perform the actual wedding ceremony.

Kai's presence at this international event was a special treat for me and Joseph's attendance was significant for Laura because he and his congregation had stood with her when she had gone through her fiercest trials and darkest valleys.

Laura was not brought down the aisle, but in eastern fashion came immediately to the front of the church. In contrast to the ceremony at the Wedding Palace, both pastors emphasized the Biblical meaning of marriage, its life-long significance and the responsibility of bringing up children in the fear and the knowledge of the Lord.

The service became a blur to me. The air was hot and sticky and my best man periodically wiped the sweat off my brow with his handkerchief.

Then came the moment when Joseph asked me, "Do you wish to take Laura as your wedded wife and love her at all times, in times of trouble and tranquillity, in times of sickness and health, in poverty and in wealth, until death do you part?"

Without hesitation, I said, "I do!"

The same question was repeated to Laura. "I do," she also said with assurance.

Joseph fixed his firm eyes on us both and stated, "I, here, in the presence of all these witnesses, now pronounce you man and wife."

He paused briefly and then added, "As a symbol of your commitment to each other, I ask you, Hannu Haukka to extend to your wife Laura a golden wedding band."

As the perspiration again formed on my brow, I lowered my extended fingers into the right pocket of my suit coat to bring forth the band of gold. But, to my horror, I couldn't find it. As my fingers desperately searched every corner of my pocket my smile turned to bewilderment and then to panic.

"I can't find the ring," I whispered hoarsely to my best man.

What a disaster!

I felt Laura's eyes mist up with disappointment. It had to be there somewhere. I had often heard stories of wedding rings rolling across the church floor. I could not foul up now. This was definitely not a time of tranquillity.

I kept on fidgeting around in my pocket, but could find nothing but balls of dust. This was supposed to be the greatest day of my life, but it was now turning into a nightmare.

Kai saw me start to stiffen up and came to my rescue.

"Take your engagement ring off your finger and give it to Laura," he whispered in Finnish.

I abandoned my search and pulled off my own engagement band and placed it on the third finger of Laura's left hand. As I did, everyone in the sanctuary sighed and laughed.

Then Joseph said in Russian, "Hannu, you may kiss your wife."

Vera, Laura's cousin who stood at my side and had interpreted the ceremony for me, translated this by saying, "You may hug your wife." So I did just that and again people laughed. I had to wait a little longer to give Laura the required kiss.

Next was the time for the reception. After unending difficulties in finding a vacant location, we located a nearby venue for the celebration. It was a place called Vesna (spring) and the manager had agreed to rent out the facility on the condition that we purchase fifty bottles of champagne. I reluctantly handed over the money for the bottles, but they never showed up for the reception. I surmised that he had a big celebration at my expense!

Laura and I were seated against the back wall of the reception hall. The guests, most of whom I had never met before, were placed at long tables that laced the room. They included Laura's relatives, Joseph's church choir and his assistants from Riga, and a few Muscovites from a musical ensemble that had unexpectedly shown up to sing at the wedding.

Because my comprehension of Russian was still limited, Laura translated the proceedings for me. Everyone who spoke wished us happiness, gave instructions on how to raise a large family, and explained how each one had to overcome the problems in his or her own marriage. Practically every speaker gave a testimony of how Jesus Christ had transformed their lives.

Of the 250 guests and restaurant personnel, I estimated that more than twenty had never been exposed to a faith in God in their personal lives. Whenever someone spoke or sang, they would turn around and stare in the direction of that person or group of singers. I could read question marks all over their faces.

Each speaker, and there was a seemingly inexhaustible line, brought forth a gift for the two of us. One of the most prized was a hand-crafted photo album of Laura and myself before we met, and also after. The snapshots were artistically laced with beautifully painted color and designs. Each page contained the most masterful artwork I had ever seen.

At one point in the proceedings, I got quite a scare. An elderly male guest from Moscow came over to our table. Leaning over to whisper something to us, he bumped the three-pronged candlestick in front of me. Before I could lift a finger, the candlestick had fallen on the table, splattering hot wax all over my black suit.

I could see the color drain from his face. He lunged for the candles in vain. The flames were out but the damage had been done. With horror in his voice, and almost weeping, he tried to utter his apologies.

The reception was almost over and it really did not matter to me whether there were spots on my suit or not and Laura and I tried to comfort him, but clearly the wedding was ruined for him.

Once everything had quieted down, and guests from far and near were on their way home, Laura and I were left alone to enjoy what remained of the evening. I turned to her and looked deep into her big beautiful blue eyes and hugged her in a long and deep embrace. Was it really true? Had the day finally arrived that we were husband and wife? There was no question that it had, and Laura looked happier than I had ever seen her.

Laura of Russia had finally become Mrs. Haukka!

Hannu and Laura, married in 1976 under the hammer and sickle.

Chapter Fifteen

KGB Calling

I stirred and reached out my arm. Yes, Laura was still there.

"Good morning," I said, as I slowly sat up in bed and rubbed the sleep from my bleary eyes.

Laura was only half awake and turned over to grasp a few more precious minutes of rest. I slipped out of bed and walked into the living room and drew open the curtains. Totally exhausted, we had slept in late. It had already been light for about three hours.

We were staying in Vera's apartment and she had discreetly moved in with a friend for the night.

I had missed the sky turning from apricot and amber to its present blue. In fact, that wonderful morning the sky had never been bluer, the sun warmer or the trees greener. For the first time, I sensed a real joy of being in Russia.

Laura eventually emerged wearing a robe and joined me at the window. We both gazed up at the heavens and held hands.

"Well, Mrs. Haukka," I asked, "how do you feel?"

With eyes brimming with joy, she replied, "I am very happy, Hannu."

As we continued to stand at the window, Laura and I were jolted back to reality by the sound of a loud knocking on the front door. I opened it and was confronted by a short, stocky, dignified man, with dark hair and bushy eyebrows. I estimated him to be about 60 years of age.

Dressed in a well-pressed blue suit, the man asked if he could come in. Although he did not present his ID, I recognized him as Colonel K. from the Karelian Division of the KGB. This man worked in the section that dealt with dissidents, religion, and other ideological phenomena alien to Communist society.

"Please draw up a chair and join us," I said as casually as I could. Colonel K. sat down in the living room and then brought out from a brown paper bag some wedding gifts: a box of candy, a bottle of champagne and a carved candlestick that I later noted had been made in India.

"May we make a toast to your happiness?" he asked in excellent English, taking hold of the champagne bottle.

"That is very kind of you," I responded. "But please excuse me. I don't drink."

The truth was that I had never even tasted alcohol. Among the many principles my wise mother had taught all of us from the earliest age was the importance of abstaining from alcohol.

"I do not understand," said the colonel, puzzled at my response. "Isn't that being a bit antisocial? I would have thought that all civilized people consumed alcoholic drinks," he added, giving a short, mirthless laugh.

"If that's the measuring stick for being civilized," I declared, trying to pick my words carefully, "then I prefer to be uncivilized."

Crestfallen, the colonel put down the bottle on the table. Evidently, he had not really stopped by to consume the "bubbly" and so the conversation shifted to more serious matters.

He had a myriad of questions. "How do you like the Soviet Union?" he then asked. "What do your Canadian friends think about the Soviet Union? Do you plan to settle in the USSR or move to the West?"

I held my lips tightly closed, but wanted to say, "What a question to ask a Canadian." Did he seriously think that I planned to move to Russia?

He continued to pepper me with leading questions. "Do your acquaintances think it will be difficult to get your wife out of the Soviet Union?" he continued.

Next came an unexpected one right out of left field. "Was there anyone from Canadian Intelligence at the wedding?" he asked, fixing his eyes on mine.

I took a deep breath. He knew he had posed an uncomfortable question. My logic told me it would be foolish and dangerous to admit meeting with Canadian Intelligence. Already, Western tourists were automatically accused of being American CIA (Central Intelligence Agency) spies.

Actually, all foreigners were potential CIA agents according to Soviet thinking. Such accusations were either intentional disinformation to discourage contacts with westerners, or extreme paranoia, common to all those in the intelligence gathering business.

Could he have known that just a short time before leaving, I had met with men from Canadian Intelligence for the first time in my life. Contrary to my common sense, I felt God's prompting to mention that incident to him. "Tell it the way it is," I felt Him telling me. "Do not attempt to dodge the question."

So I told Colonel K. that I had met up with these officers. His interest was now piqued.

"When anyone from the Soviet Union travels abroad," I continued, "what are they required to do when they return home? You ask for a report," I pressed on, answering my own question. "That is a well-known fact. The same applies with me. I have been to the Soviet Union some twenty times and I was to be married to a Soviet citizen."

"They wanted to know how I was doing and if I had encountered any problems from your people."

The colonel was, by now, all ears. "What did you tell them?" he asked intrigued. "Have you had any difficulties?"

"Well no," I responded. "Not yet! But they did offer to help me if I did encounter any trouble in getting Laura out of the country."

The elderly KGB officer interjected. No," he stated, "you won't need to turn to them for help. "There will be no difficulties. I don't believe that there will be problems in obtaining an exit permit for your wife."

With that, he rose to his feet and repeated that there would be no interference from the Soviet authorities.

"Perhaps the difficulties will come from another source," he added cryptically.

I did not grasp what he was hinting at. With that, he politely excused himself and left. I was perplexed not knowing what to make of his parting comment about "another source."

* * * * *

I came down to earth with a bump when I realized that that evening I would have to leave Laura. My Soviet visa was due to expire and I was obligated to be at Soviet customs the following evening.

Laura packed some sandwiches and accompanied me to the train to Leningrad from where I would have to travel alone back to Helsinki. She was in a somber mood, as we stood by the side of the stationary Soviet Railways train that was about to depart for the West.

As the Russian countryside had flashed by our windows, we had talked intensively about what lay ahead. Now, finally, the moment came for me to bid my wife good-bye. She climbed on board with me and helped me to find a seat. I put a bag on it to reserve my place, then walked with Laura to the carriage door. We hugged each other and kissed for a brief moment.

"I am going to miss you," Laura said in halting whisper that struggled for breath.

"I will miss you, too," I repeated softly.

Twilight was gathering as the train lightly jerked into life and Laura broke into a run alongside the coach until she could no longer keep up with the building momentum of the train, all the while looking at me with sadness in her beautiful dark blue eyes.

Tears stung my eyes as I could no longer see her. My thoughts scurried round in frantic circles, as I already began to long for her.

"God, please take care of Laura until we meet again," I whispered. "Please let me see her again!"

Chapter Sixteen

The Cross And The Bolshevik

For Russia's millions of believers, this was to be a celebration where they could commemorate the 100 year anniversary of the translation of the Bible into their own language.

The history of the Russian Bible dates back to the middle of the ninth century. Slavic scholars, Kirill and Methodus, prepared a translation of the Psalms in a language understandable to a degree, to the people of the kingdom of Rus—today's Ukrainian city of Kiev.

Then, a half century later a translation of the Septuagint was completed in old Slavonic Russian. But it was not until 1703 that the translation of the Bible into spoken Russian commenced. Czar Peter The First gave Pastor Glyuk the task of doing this much needed translation. Sadly, Glyuk died two years later with the job incomplete.

Later in 1815, Czar Aleksander The First, returning home from a trip to western Europe, ordered the Holy Synod of the Russian Orthodox Church to produce a Bible translation readable by the common folk in the language of the people. In 1822, the first books were released. After Aleksander's death, however, the books were destroyed by fire and the translation largely lost.

Finally, in 1876, a complete one-volume Bible in the Synodal translation was published. It is the translation still used to this day.

Christian leaders from the West had been invited by pastors in the Soviet Union to attend different events to celebrate this completion of the Russian Bible.

So it was with great excitement in August of 1976, that I joined a group of Norwegian and Finnish pastors and leaders who had been invited by Joseph Bondarenko to take part in the celebration in Riga.

We booked into the Hotel Riga. Laura had decided to stay with friends who were members of Bondarenko's church.

Before going out into the street to make contact with Valeri and Laura, I had been met by Galina, an Intourist guide who had singled me out for special instructions.

"You do not have permission to leave the city for even a moment," she warned me. "Your visa is only good for Riga. Do you understand me?"

I understood better than she knew. Six months previously I had dealt a devastating blow to one Intourist guide by saying she had allowed us to leave the city limits without her guidance.

This guide had obviously been told about the incident, and did not intend to make the same mistake.

Galina, however, made a different one. She assumed that I was the leader of the group and having warned me, she thought she had warned the whole party.

The festival was scheduled to be held at a church outside the city limits.

I was not only glad to be back in Riga for these wonderful celebrations, but also because it meant I would be reunited briefly with Laura, who had traveled to Riga to act as an interpreter for us. We had agreed to rendezvous by the statue of

119

Lenin in the main square surrounded by a garden, across the street from the Communist bookstore.

As we waited for Laura to arrive, we all went into the political bookstore to check out the latest propaganda put out by Novesti Press. I was amused to also see anti-American posters hung on the wall. Uncle Sam was definitely not someone who was admired by the leaders of the USSR and he was parodied as a symbol of Western aggression, clutching a fistful of missiles in his hands and spewing forth hatred for what he saw as "The Evil Empire."

LENIN AND A TAXI CAB

Wondering where Laura was, I stepped out the door of the store and admired the spectacular view of Lenin, with his right arm outstretched as if he was hailing a taxi cab. The joke in the Soviet Union was that taxis were so difficult to stop, that he was forever holding out his hand.

Across the street, I noticed a church with a large cross on its dome. From my angle, it appeared that Lenin was actually holding the cross in his hand.

"I don't think they planned for that when they erected the statue," I chuckled to a Finnish friend who stood beside me. I heard later that when the authorities eventually realized the symbolism, they ordered the removal of the cross from the church dome.

Still, there was no sign of my wife, so I occupied my time observing the gray Ladas limp along the street past the statue. Then I spotted the uninvited company we had. We were under surveillance.

Across the street, a little way up from the bookstore, stood a man and woman who were glancing our way frequently enough to arouse my suspicion. What made them stand out was that everyone else appeared to be going someplace, but they were going nowhere.

When they saw that I was looking directly at them, they tried to cover their tracks by ducking into a phone booth.

"They are pretending to dial a number, but notice how they keep watching us," I pointed out to my friend. Sam, another one of our delegation, who had by now stepped into the street, realized what was taking place. So he took out his Super 8 mm camera and pointed it at them and pressed the record button.

Just then, Laura arrived with Valeri. I spotted the pair standing across the intersection, waiting for the lights to turn green. When it did, people surged into the road from both sides of the street.

Seconds later, Laura was in my arms. I hugged my wife and told her how much I had missed her. She smiled and repeated that she, too, had missed me. I looked into her eyes and saw a kind of peace and joy that I had not detected before our marriage.

Valeri extended his hand for a firm grip by me. "We have a lot of attention," he said cautiously, referring to our shadows.

"Yes, I had noticed," I told him. "Let's move off into the park," I suggested.

"Please be ready by 9:00 a.m. and there will be two Ladas waiting for you," he said.

Preempting police action, Bondarenko had instructed his drivers to take the visitors to the church service by taking back roads, which resembled dirt paths more than roads. This detour was taken to try to evade potential police roadblocks, and indeed these had been set up at all major intersections.

I was under house arrest by my Intourist guide, but the others climbed into a small fleet of Ladas, (the most popular Soviet brand of auto), and they bumped their way through a forest and over a track in a field. After these considerable evasive maneuvers, the Ladas stopped in a wooded area, about 100 yards from the church. I was told later that our travelers were enjoying the cat-and-mouse activities of our drivers.

I had not bothered to tell the others about the prohibition against leaving the city limits. Besides, it was the responsibility of Intourist to make sure that everyone received the "stay inside the city" information, I reasoned.

They joined in a wonderful service led by Joseph. Along with a huge choir they sang heartily the great hymns of the church and listened to a powerful sermon about the importance of God's Word by Bondarenko, as Laura sat by translating his words for the group.

The delegation was all fired up as they returned to the hotel to recount what had occurred. Some exuberantly discussed the adventure of their trip. Everyone was obviously challenged by the courage and dedication of the Soviet believers as they served God in such trying circumstances.

"He is definitely number one in their lives," one of them told me.

Our itinerary called for us to return to Helsinki via Leningrad. Laura again came to the station, and ran alongside the train as it pulled away from the platform. Soviet Railways had its own agenda, which called for an early arrival in Leningrad.

The night train ride would take us again through the frontier settlement of Viborg. Viborg had been a Finnish city before the close of the Second World War. The advancing Soviet army had driven the Finns almost 100 miles west of the western frontier.

After hostilities ceased, the borders were redrawn. Finland retained its independence, but lost a lot of territory on its eastern flank. Viborg was only twenty miles from the new boundary. Practically all Finns had fled the war zone and were soon replaced by a majority of Russians.

Because of the slightly-after-midnight schedule, tourists were usually sound asleep when the train pulled into the Viborg station.

"Passports please," barked the uniformed Russian guard. Sharing the compartment with me was my younger brother Jyrki, who had come all the way from Canada for his first visit behind the ominous Iron Curtain.

The border police had quietly worked their way down the coach to our compartment. There was a light knock on the door. We were the first in our party to be inspected.

Two officers began systematically going through our baggage. They were obviously looking for something in particular. They lifted our mattress, where I had been lying, rummaged through our suitcases, opened the radiator and even checked the air conditioning.

After checking everything, I understood enough Russian to understand when one of them said, "It's not here!"

I wondered to myself what was "not here." By the time they had gotten to the next compartment, I finally figured out what they were searching for.

In the next compartment, were two members of our delegation: Eino Ahonen and Heikki Lahti. They were respected members of the Finnish Pentecostal movement. The trip had proved too much for them. Both were first timers to the USSR and were dead tired after the exciting events of the trip. They had not noticed that the train had stopped and was now at Soviet customs. With them was Sam with his camera.

One of the soldiers knocked on the door. It was a noticeably heavier knock than we had received. The impatient officer rattled the door and found that it was locked from the inside.

"Customs control!" he yelled. "Open up."

There was still no reaction from inside. Suddenly, the soldier lost his patience. Bracing himself against the offending coach wall opposite the compartment, he lifted his right leg waist high. Then the knee-high black leather boot thundered full force against the compartment door again and again so hard that the walls of the compartment shuddered violently.

"I said customs! Open the door" he continued to roar.

By this time, no one in the coach was sleeping. Finally there was a response. I held my breath as I heard a shuffling inside the next compartment.

"Sorry," I could clearly hear in Finnish. "Don't worry. I am opening the door."

I heard the soldier command the inhabitants to come out and stand in the hall. The clergymen tried to stall, so they could pull on their trousers. But the soldiers did not want to wait for such niceties.

I slid open the door and saw the sorry sight of these respected leaders standing in the hallway in their briefs. Seeing the humorous side of the incident, I realized they had never enrolled in a fitness program as they stood there in only their underwear.

The clamor had brought some Polish tourists into the corridor and they began cursing the Soviet soldiers for their boorishness in words that are not fit to repeat.

As my colleagues stood there shivering, the soldiers moved into the compartment and ransacked their belongings. The brethren were then called, one by one, for additional inspection. Heikki Lahti had purchased a padded coffeepot warmer in the form of a Matroshka doll. It was a delightful souvenir, but the inspecting agent decided that it looked "suspicious."

The stuffing of the doll was obviously not accessible. It had been sewn tight at the factory in Riga. This did not deter the soldier. He drew out his military knife and, with its long blade, sliced open the lower edge of the warmer. He found stuffing. The warmer was little use after that.

It was definitely an iron fist operation. The scare factor was enough to cause further complications with the Finns. One of the party ended up sitting on his cot, after opening the window, and began consuming his heart tablets.

As the search continued, one of the officers came across Sam's films.

"What are these?" questioned the customs agent, pointing to the thirteen films in Sam's camera case.

"These are film of our trip to Riga," he explained.

The agent took hold of the films and spread them out on the cot before him. He wanted to discover if they were pictures of an "anti-Soviet" nature. The films were of great value to us. Sam had shot footage of the festivities of the anniversary of the Russian Bible. They were extremely valuable, but Sam was so intimidated that he expressed his willingness to hand them over.

I realized there was only a slim hope of saving the films. I made a last ditch attempt to save them before they were forfeited forever.

I rushed out from my compartment and into theirs. "The films are mine," I affirmed. "You may confiscate them only against a receipt."

The Russian agent eyed me doubtfully. But, I had been across Soviet borders many times, and had learned a thing or two about such situations.

As a Canadian citizen, I knew I had the possibility of asking my government to intervene and request that the confiscated material be returned. I knew that the Canadian Embassy in Moscow would be more willing to act than the Finnish authorities, who were ever conscious of not upsetting their powerful neighbor.

"Sit down," screamed the officer as he began frantically scribbling. "Here is your receipt."

"I will be back in the Soviet Union via this checkpoint next week," I said. "Can I pick up the films then?"

"Sure," he said, "just present this paper and ask for them."

The customs officer then left with the offending films stuffed in his pocket.

When the train finally arrived in Helsinki, the problems we had encountered had been recounted to Eino, my boss at the publishing house. He was definitely not pleased with the news.

"PACK YOUR BAGS AND LEAVE"

Outside the train station as we waited for our ride, Eino spoke words that caused havoc in my young soul. "Let me give you a piece of advice, Hannu," he said, not showing much sensitivity, "pack your bags now and go back to Canada. Just leave Russia alone."

It was as if my heart had been smashed into a thousand pieces.

I was overcome with a feeling of black despair at how quickly my world had fallen apart. But what I didn't realize at the time was that God was using this negative situation to temper my soul so that it would endure the pressures that I was sure to encounter in the ministry in the coming years.

Chapter Seventeen

Farewell, Mother Russia

I was again on the train back to Leningrad and then onto Laura's home city. Up until that point we had only been together for a grand total of two days after our wedding.

When the train stopped at the Soviet customs, an officer came into my carriage and I immediately presented him with a receipt for the films that had been previously confiscated. The official took hold of one end of the receipt and I held on to the other. We began to play a game of tug-of-war which he won. Victoriously, he took hold of the piece of paper and slipped it into his pocket.

"You will not need this receipt," he said. "You'll get the films on your way out."

"Hey, wait a minute," I protested. "You can't do that! This is ridiculous. I can't guarantee that you will be on duty when I return." No one had seen him pocket my receipt so I knew that, in effect, it no longer existed.

"Trust the Soviet Union," he smirked as he made his way out of my carriage and into the one next door. I scratched my head at his actions. *It cannot be possible,* I mused to myself. Actually, it could! Everything was possible in this country.

"Okay, so round one is yours," I muttered to myself.

When I returned to Helsinki, I sent a letter of protest to the chief of customs in Viborg and also to the Canadian Department of External Affairs in Ottawa. But it seemed that this was futile and I would never see the films again.

Laura stood patiently at Petrozavodsk station waiting for the Leningrad train to pull in. As I disembarked, I spotted her and quickly jumped down onto the platform, dropped my luggage, and gave her a deep, long kiss.

"I am going to stay here with you until you get your exit papers and we can leave together," I told my wife. "Well, Hannu," she told me as we headed for the exit, "I have filed for my exit. So I guess all we can do is to pray and wait patiently!"

Colonel K. would apparently play a key role in the process of Laura's exit visa. Her dossier was, after all, in his jurisdiction. His promise that there would be no road blocks was off little comfort. The KGB was not an agency noted for telling the truth. Neither was it that agency's business to render assistance to believers. Our trust was in God alone.

I was able to stay at Laura's home because my visa had been processed on the basis of a personal invitation by Laura. In such cases, if the Soviets issued a visa, it released the traveler of the obligation of residing in a hotel, which would have been expensive over a period of the three months that I had planned to stay.

There were never any doubts in our minds that we had not made a mistake in getting married. To us, the impossible had already happened when Laura had received her visitor's visa for Finland. We had taken this as a sign from God. Being together with Laura in Russia, was infinitely much better for me that being alone in far away Finland.

* * * * *

Perhaps our best guarded secret was our intent to join Earl Poysti and his radio ministry in Austria. Earl was the most respected and loved radio voice amongst Christians in the USSR. The KGB considered him a menace to their ideological interests. We had made plans to travel on to Austria soon after our arrival in Finland. No one in Russia was aware of our plan—or so we thought.

We had made sure that no one had overheard our plans by only discussing them out of doors, and only between the two of us. This action was to lessen the risk of the authorities finding out that we would be working with a man who was hated by the Soviet authorities for penetrating the Iron Curtain with the Gospel message. The State was not interested in allowing its citizens to travel abroad to work for organizations that they so disdained.

One evening in late fall, about a month before our hoped for departure, we received Colonel K. at Laura's home. He had requested the meeting by leaving a conspicuous envelope in her mailbox. The letter had requested that Laura call a certain telephone number. She phoned the number and he had suggested the day, time and place, for the get-together.

As we sipped tea together, the convivial KGB officer unexpectedly said something that jolted both Laura and myself. "When you leave the USSR, you will be going to work with Earl Poysti," he stated.

I stared at him in disbelief. "When you arrive in Austria, a home will be ready for you. It will be in a two-story building and you will have the upper floor." The Colonel was telling me things that even I did not know. The KGB had lived up to its reputation for thoroughness.

All I could surmise was that they had monitored my calls to Austria while I was in Finland, or had intercepted and read the mail I had received from Poysti. Even so, that did not explain where Colonel K. had picked up the information about our apartment.

"Perhaps," I told Laura after he had left, "either they have assigned agents in Austria to provide a profile on Earl Poysti's ministry or there is a mole in Earl's organization." The meeting caused considerable anxiety in my spirit. The KGB apparently knew of our closely guarded secret. Would this information sabotage our plans to leave Russia? Maybe they would let us go for a price, or would they attempt to pressure us into collaborating with them?

We met with the Colonel on two further occasions during my three month residence in Petrozavodsk. The last meeting proved to be the most extraordinary.

"You will soon be moving to the West," he said as he looked directly at me. "In everything that you do and say, I want you to remember one thing," he went on, fixing a stern eye on me. "Remember that we have been good to Laura. Things could have worked out a lot differently. We have enough evidence on file against her to lock her up for many years. But we haven't done so. We have been kind instead!"

He was, of course, referring to Laura's arrest in Riga and the literature that was forwarded to his office by the KGB in Riga. Both Laura, many others and I, had wondered why there had been total silence in Petrozavodsk. Someone had obviously pulled a blanket over the case. That someone, we were discovering, was Colonel K.

After a long, deliberate pause, he continued, "We have been good to Laura," he stated. "Never forget that when you talk about the USSR abroad."

Then he leaned forward in his chair and gave Laura some personal advice. "When you leave the USSR, you will have a guardian angel wherever you go. But, should the need arise, that guardian angel will change into a demon and we will find you, wherever you may be!"

For some unknown reason, Laura's visa was being held up. The local authorities readily extended my visa originally issued for one month, allowing me to stay an extra two. The extension gave them an opportunity to meet with me and form an opinion about me. They wanted to find out if I was a potential source of information that continuously appeared in publications in the West, claiming that Christians were being persecuted in the Soviet Union.

Pipelines obviously existed. One example was Keston College in England, who were constantly publicizing stories about Christians being arrested and put on trial for their counterrevolutionary activities. This was proving embarrassing for the government who had instructed the KGB to find out the sources and to plug up these pipelines.

On one occasion, Laura and I were approached by a man called Valeri, who was suspected to be a KGB informant. He invited us to an unregistered service to be held in the city. Valeri had been too persistent, to the point were he aroused our suspicion. Laura and I decided not to attend, but Laura's mother did. The meeting was raided by the militia. Believers were dragged to waiting police vehicles through the snow with no shoes on. The owner of the house was heavily fined and the pastor was arrested, but later released.

Valeri later came to see us. He played an audio recording he had made that sent chills up and down my spine. I heard the commanding officer yelling and in the background I could clearly hear babies crying. Then I listened to tables and chairs being overturned as the police forcibly dragged the men out of the service. I then heard a guitar being smashed and women protesting the actions of the police.

He handed me the tape. "Please take it to the West," he insisted. My first reaction was that this was hot stuff. Suspecting foul play, Laura turned him down. Her suspicions were correct. A few years later, I learned that Valeri had denied his faith and became a drunk. He had been a KGB mole in the church.

* * * * *

It was already December 10. Laura's exit visa was due to expire within a week. If Laura was not out of the country by midnight on December 17, she would have to start the bureaucratic process again from scratch. Laura's exit had now been approved by the Soviet authorities, but the Finns were now, for some unexplainable reason, dragging their feet in granting her an entry visa. Difficulties from another source — those haunting words of Colonel K. returned to me. The implications were spooky. Did the KGB have a man inside Finnish State Security to slow down the process?

After a hair-raising wait and the intervention of Canadian authorities, the necessary permit from Finland came through, and not a moment too soon. A sizable crowd of well-wishers had gathered at the railway station to say good-bye to us both. It was a historic moment for her church. One of their own was leaving for freedom. For Laura, the experience was tinged with sorrow. Her loved ones and everything dear to her would be left behind. She had no idea if she would ever set foot in her hometown again.

There was not much to take along with her. Her possessions were scanty to say the least. In all, we had two suitcases and a homemade wooden box, two feet by three feet, that I had slapped together in a few hours. In the box was a dinner set we had received as a gift from Joseph Bondarenko's church.

As the train approached the Russian-Finnish border, I looked down at my watch. It was 11:45 p.m., which meant that there was only fifteen minutes to go on Laura's exit visa. I let out a deep sigh of relief and thanked the Lord for his faithfulness. He had kept his eye on us. Real guardian angels of light had been at work, paving the way for this grand exit. At last, we were leaving Mother Russia.

Well known Russian radio personalities, Earl and Pirkko Poysti. Earl provided the early training mandatory for the events to come.

Chapter Eighteen

Guardians Of The Soviet Empire

There was one thing for certain. We would have a white Christmas in Helsinki. As the train slowly glided into the station, snowflakes were gently drifting down from the gray sky and blanketing the floor in a welcoming carpet for us.

Our stay in Helsinki lasted for only two weeks. We were enroute to Austria where we were to join Earl Poysti in his ministry to the Soviet Union. The studio was located in a small alpine village in eastern Austria.

Veteran radio evangelist, Poysti, was born in Ussuriisk, Siberia, in 1920. His father, Nikolai, was a missionary who had been born in St. Petersburg. The family moved to Harbin, Manchuria, China, to escape from the advancing Bolshevik troops. From there, the family moved to New York where, in 1946, Nikolai launched a radio ministry to Russia. Earl moved into his father's place of ministry before his father's death. He was soon to become the most listened to radio voice on short-wave in the whole of the Soviet Union.

He was a gifted preacher and linguist, speaking Russian better than any of the other international ministers that I knew of. His soothing voice was enjoyable to listen to and his pronunciation was exceptionally clear and accent free.

If Earl was the mighty voice over the airwaves, Pirkko, his wonderful wife and mother of their ten children, was a brilliant administrator who held everything together and kept things running smoothly. She had exceptional diplomatic skills and an uncanny knack for ironing out problems that arose from time to time in the ministry and also in the family home.

Because of her academic studies and her excellent command of the Russian language, Laura's job was to proofread all of Earl's sermons. He would write them out on paper, and she would then make all the grammatical corrections. As somebody fresh out of the country, she would give Earl cultural orientation on conditions in the USSR. This was important for a preacher of the Gospel who could not freely travel to meet his target audience.

Laura also created a new program called "Songs of Praise" where Russian Christians could write and request and dedicate any Christian song to a friend or relative. This rapidly became a very popular program.

I was the recording technician responsible for the technical work and editing of the studio's five radio programs every week.

Laura and I soon settled into our apartment in Austria and I was spooked to see that our new home was exactly as Colonel K. had described it.

All was going well, but Laura was finding the move to the West a radical change. Although the local stores were full of goods and the staff at the Poysti headquarters were most kind, by June, Laura was overcome by homesickness.

"I need to go back to Russia for a visit," she told me. "I really miss it."

Out of the blue, we received an invitation to attend the wedding of Valeri, Bondarenko's assistant, who had been the best man at my wedding. We applied for visas to travel to Riga, where the happy occasion was to take place and were surprised when they were granted by the Soviet Embassy in Vienna.

The Baltic Sea was as smooth as a mirror, as the MS Tallinn cruised for the three-and-a-half hour journey across from Helsinki harbor to the Estonian port city of Tallinn.

As we approached Tallinn, I began to silently pray for Laura's safety. I was tormented by the anticipation that my wife could encounter problems as she had packed her bag with Bibles and other Christian literature. I had reasoned with her that she was still a Soviet citizen and, if she was caught smuggling this "anti-Soviet" material, she could be arrested and swallowed up by the Gulag.

"Hannu, I know the needs of my own country," she told me with a high flush in her face. "I cannot return to Russia empty-handed."

Laura reminded me of the numerous hand-written New Testaments and Gospels that Christians used on a daily basis.

"Where else will they get a portion of Scripture?" she asked me. "They need spiritual food in order to grow and remain strong in the faith."

I reluctantly had to agree with her.

The customs hall, a one-story building divided into three sections, was not big by international standards, but it provided a big hurdle to cross. We carried our bags through the Plexiglas doors and lined up for the daunting customs inspection.

Each passenger lifted their bags up onto the counter and was then asked to open up them for inspection by the customs officer. I watched nervously as these men, dressed in two-piece dull green uniforms, black shoes, and gold stars on their shoulders that indicated their rank, scrutinized passengers evenbefore they stepped up to the counter. After numerous visits, I knew they could detect with surprising accuracy, restlessness, nervousness, and unnatural behavior.

There was no X-ray scanning equipment in service at the time. Laura and I simultaneously laid our baggage on the counter. I, once again, shot up a telegram prayer to God for the eyes of the guard to be blinded.

As he began his search of Laura's luggage, the man suddenly spotted a copy of the Helsinki Daily News that Laura had brought with her as reading material on the boat ride. He dug his claws into this "hot item" and rushed it over to the supervising commander for approval before it could be returned to its owner.

He got an affirmative nod and returned with a smile covering his face and announced to my wife, "You may keep it."

Meanwhile, her bag that was stuffed with Christian materials, lay unattended on the counter. The paper had distracted the officer and he did not check her any further.

As she picked up her belongings, I stepped towards her and hissed, "Let's go." I could have screamed as I said this, but knew this would arouse suspicion.

I read the agitation that flashed in Laura's eyes. She really did not need my help, but nothing seemed amiss to the officer. As we proceeded to passport and visa control, I wanted to let out a whoop of jubilation, silently, of course. I thought I would burst at the seams with joy because of the spectacular way God had blinded the eyes of the Soviet border guard.

Behind passport control there was the public sector for people to meet incoming visitors. Beyond that there was a small parking lot for taxis, buses and private vehicles.

We were met there by a member of Joseph's church who drove us in his humble Lada to the Hotel Riga, where we had a reservation.

The wedding service was a time of sheer joy for all of us gathered in that underground church. As the congregation's voice welled to sing praises to God, I turned to look at Laura, and saw her face bathed in smiles as she was again experiencing the spiritual roots she had longed for in the West.

Joseph Bondarenko, after pronouncing the couple "man and wife," proceeded to preach the Gospel to all those attending. Weddings in the Soviet Union were also an evange-

135

listic event. The KGB could hardly interfere with the outreach that was directed more at the unchurched than the bride and groom.

Laura soaked in every minute of the fellowship with her brothers and sisters in the Lord. This was home for her. How she had longed to worship, sing and pray together one more time with her Russian friends.

* * * * *

Laura's mother, Eva, was quietly reading her Bible, when an insistent knock came on the door of her apartment in Petrozavodsk. She went to the door and was confronted by a young man who turned out to be a messenger from the KGB. This incident had taken place a month before our visit to Riga.

"This is for you," he announced as he handed her a box, bound together with string.

She thanked him and took the package inside. The packet contained Sam's films.

Vera had transported them to Riga. She handed them to us, and although I was delighted to see them again, I felt a check in my spirit. I understood how powerful the KGB network was. A regional headquarters, a thousands miles from the border, could request practically anything from customs and have them obey.

We were due to fly back to Helsinki through Leningrad and I was already worrying about what could happen at the airport. I was fully aware that I could not hide the films.

My fears were fully justified. At customs at the Leningrad airport, the officer immediately spied the box of films that I was carrying and took them from my custody.

"These films were returned and have been cleared by the authorities," I protested. "If you don't believe me, call your colleagues in Petrozavodsk."

I knew by the man's stony gaze that I was losing this battle. Not only did he have the films, but he also had confiscated ten magnificent photographs I had been given of a baptismal service in the heart of Russia.

Without explanation, the man disappeared, apparently to place a call to someone either at Viborg customs or to the KGB.

Ten minutes later he reappeared with the box of films. Without saying a word, he handed the films back to me.

"What about the pictures?" I asked tentatively.

"I will keep them," he responded.

Laura and I then made our way to the waiting Finnair DC-9 aircraft. As we walked towards the gate, I felt relieved to have made it through customs with so little commotion.

"It could have been worse," I whispered to Laura.

As we took our seats, side by side, at the rear of the plane, we fastened our seatbelts. The plane was full and I was thankful that a film of a baptismal service that hung from a string under my shirt had not been discovered.

I glanced at my watch and noted that the departure was delayed. An uneasiness set in. Just then, the front door of the aircraft swung open. The appearance of a Red Army soldier caused me to freeze in my seat. He was apparently trying to locate a passenger. His sweeping gaze located the person he was looking for. He pointed toward me and signaled me to come forward.

My heart throbbed wildly in my chest. What did he want? Had customs changed their mind and were they planning to repossess the thirteen movie films? Or had they decided to pull me out for a more thorough inspection? I knew if they did I would lose the special jewels hanging from my neck. There was no way I could unload it.

Reluctantly, I unbuckled my seatbelt.

"Why, Lord?" I asked. "Why?"

As I stood up, I turned to look at Laura. She had fear written all over her face. The walk up to the front of the American manufactured aircraft seemed never ending. As I approached the soldier, I noticed he seemed to be more shaken than I was.

His hairdo was messed up. Somewhere between the terminal and the plane he had lost his hat. In his outstretched hands were the confiscated black and white photographs of the baptism. He handed them back to me — one by one — as if to make sure that I saw all of them.

I could not believe what I was seeing. The almighty Soviet customs had humbled itself to cater to a lone tourist. There had to be an explanation.

A Finnair flight attendant smiled at me as I quickly returned to my seat.

The jet arched westward toward Helsinki and I presented the pictures to Laura for her inspection. My heartbeat was slowly returning to normal.

Chapter Nineteen

A Taste of
Persecution

The conditions could not have been worse on the Baltic Sea on that February day in 1977 when Sune Olofoson, a reporter for the largest daily newspaper in Sweden, and Eric, a Swedish Christian, and I were traveling back to the Soviet Union. Extraordinarily low temperatures had caused the ice to form even thicker than usual. I watched in awe through a window as the MS Tallinn, forged its way through the ice that had been broken up by Finnish ice-breakers.

As we entered international waters, the channel that had been previously thrashed out by the huge Finnish ice-crunching vessels, suddenly solidified. To complicate matters, strong winds that had been blowing all night, had wedged the marine ice-fields so tight that the channel had disappeared and was no longer navigable.

As we entered the denser concentration of ice I could feel the ship lose speed and eventually grind to a halt. We had been trapped by massive sheets of ice surrounding the boat for as far as the eye could see.

Then the captain ordered that the ship be put into reverse and the engines roared as the ship doubled back on its tracks. Momentarily, the ship again lurched forward to gain only about fifty yards in the frozen slabs of water.

The maneuver was repeated about a half a dozen times before the ship came to a final rest hopelessly jammed in a mass of solid ice in the middle of nowhere.

The trip, which normally took three hours from Finland to Soviet Estonia, dragged on for twenty-seven hours. We could have made it to the Soviet Union faster by walking across the ice-fields, but that was impossible. The punishing temperature would have halted any tourist within 100 yards of the boat.

The icebreaker ultimately arrived, cutting us loose from our icy bonds, putting us at our destination one day late.

We were due to attend an unregistered church service in a private home in a little town outside Riga. After checking into the hotel, we headed for the town. At 10:00 a.m., when the meeting began, the house was jammed with at least 150 worshippers.

The faces of those who attended reflected a devotion that I had rarely encountered in the West. Their devoted worship made me long to be in heaven, where it would be like this all the time. As is usual during a service in the Soviet Union, there were a succession of preachers who opened up the Bible to those present.

At 2:00 p.m., as the service was in full swing, I heard the ominous sound of a car pulling up in the yard.

"It's the police," said one of the believers to Sune, who quickly scrambled up to the attic of the house from where he clicked away at the militiamen with his Nikkormat through a window. *What a scoop*, he thought, *this would be for the daily newspaper in Stockholm*.

For reasons unknown, the militia unexpectedly left the premises without entering the service.

Sune reentered the room and the service continued without interruption. Joseph Bondarenko stood up to give an altar call. About a dozen people responded by standing up and requesting prayer. Each was asked whether he or she was prepared to "pay the price" for this life-changing decision to follow Jesus Christ in the atheistic Soviet Union.

Among those who made a commitment that afternoon was a young man called Anatoly Smolyak. Eleven years later, Anatoly would be the first Russian to join our television ministry as a cameraman.

A couple of hours later, the service was over and many had stayed behind for a time of informal fellowship, during which we were interrupted by a breathless young man.

"The police have set up roadblocks at the all of the intersections leading to the town," he announced hoarsely. "They are checking all the cars and have muzzled police dogs on hand."

Sune and I exchanged concerned glances as the messenger continued, "They are looking for Hannu. They will be here within a few minutes."

Bondarenko wasted no time. He ordered us westerners to gather up our coats and belongings. "Empty your pockets of all letters, messages and cassettes," he added urgently.

Sune unloaded his films and handed them to a Russian brother standing close by. With that, we stepped outside. Joseph had summoned Tolya, a local believer, to be our escort.

"He knows the terrain like the back of his hand," said Joseph Bondarenko.

"See those trees behind the house? Head for them!" Tolya instructed.

He took us through the woods, thereby missing the roadblocks. As we headed across the snow-covered field in the direction of the trees, a set of headlights appeared on a nearby road lighting up the terrain.

CROSS-COUNTRY RUN

At that precise moment, Eric toppled headlong into the snow. He was overweight and was in no shape for the unscheduled cross-country run.

"Get up Eric," Sune, my journalist friend hollered breathlessly. "The police have come."

141

Desperately gasping for oxygen, Eric, still lying full length in the snow, reached out his arms to grab Sune's coat like a drowning man.

"You're crazy," Eric screamed in frustration. "We can't outrun the police. I'm going back to hand myself in."

Sune was not planning to surrender that easily. He grabbed Eric by the shoulder and heaved him to his feet. Breathing heavily, Eric floundered his way into the woods.

By this time, another patrol car had arrived on the scene and was also illuminating the darkness with its headlights. I could clearly hear one of the policeman say, "The Westerners must be in there somewhere."

We were fortunate to have Tolya with us. He could recognize every mound, field, tree and trail, even though it was now dark and the ground covered in banks of snow. Skillfully, he led us along a white path to a nearby village. None of us were equipped with winter boots. We had come dressed for a church service, not a run through the snow. Even though my dress shoes were already full of snow, I wasn't about to complain.

We approached a bleak-looking village which consisted of a dozen log houses and no more than four streets. The main "drag" appeared to end at the railway tracks, forming a "T" intersection. The roads were covered in knee-deep snow. A snow plough, I surmised, had not been through in days, perhaps weeks.

Only a four-wheel drive could get through here, I thought to myself. Of course, I was aware that no one in the USSR owned such a vehicle at that time. At that precise moment, two beams of light flashed around the corner.

"Jump for the ditch," shouted Tolya in Russian.

"Hit the ditch," I repeated to my exhausted friends in English.

I dove for the ditch, stomach first. A brief moment later, a military Jeep-like vehicle passed by us, whipping up a blizzard in its wake. We all lay still, hardly breathing. Tolya wanted to make sure that there was not a second vehicle following close by. There was not!

"The danger is over," I heard Tolya finally say as he motioned us out of the ditch.

We huddled together for a brief moment of prayer. We needed to cross the tracks without being detected. About a hundred yards down the tracks was a railway crossing. There, we could see a checkpoint with searchlights and dogs barking at the end of their chains. It seemed that there was nowhere for us to go.

Despite the freezing weather, Tolya removed his thick fur hat, closed his eyes and crossed his hands in prayer.

"Heavenly Father," he began, his breath clearly visible in the freezing air, "thank you for protecting us from that patrol car. Now I ask that You take us over the tracks to safety. Please take us to our destination. I pray this in the name of the Father, Son and Holy Spirit. Amen." We all shouted a hearty "Amen" with him.

We agreed to attempt to cross all at one time, walking shoulder to shoulder, so that we could not be individually counted and so that from a hundred yards away, we would appear as one man. The police were on alert for the four of us so that was our camouflage.

As we stepped over the tracks, I glanced in the direction of the crossing. I could see the police, searchlights, dogs and cars. We descended the slope on the other side of the long shafts of iron.

We had not been spotted.

LEADER OF THE PACK

Tolya continued to be the leader of the pack as we traipsed through the snowy forest to a predesignated spot along the Riga highway, well clear of the checkpoints.

We had successfully avoided the police dragnet, but Joseph's chauffeur, who had been sent through the roadblock to pick us up and take us to our hotel, had not made it through. They had outfoxed us by arresting the driver for no apparent reason.

We would have waited for our ride forever had Tolya not informed us of his suspicions. Fortunately, he had a contingency plan. We were very fortunate as a taxi headed our way on the snowbound road. Tolya rushed onto the highway and flagged it down. The driver counted our party and indicated that there was one too many.

We were shocked when he refused to take any of us and sped away into the night, leaving us standing there on the snowy highway.

Time was, by now, running out. I was aware that our Intourist guide would be waiting for us at the hotel. The departure time of our night train to Leningrad was closing in on us.

We were out in the middle of nowhere and I was already unpopular with the KGB.

"Let's pray for another taxi," I suggested in desperation.

We bowed our heads and I implored the Lord to help us. Soon, another taxi arrived, but the driver again hesitated to take us on board.

"Five is too many," he barked.

In desperation, I suggested that I lay down on the laps of the big Swedes so that only three heads would show in the back seat.

"We will give you a big tip as well," I added.

That clinched the deal and he sped off towards the hotel in Riga with me spread-eagled over the knees of my friends. We were out of the woods and on our way out of the country.

Chapter Twenty

"Death To The Pigs"

God never promised to give me a problem-free ministry or an obstacle-free walk with Him. He promised to be with me in my dark valleys and take me through them.

From Russia, Laura and I had moved to Austria. For about six months, we had enjoyed ministry to Russia by radio at Earl's side. Also, my home church had been excited about us joining his ministry. Now, however, I was in Earl's office in Stockholm not expecting the thunderbolt that was about to hit me.

His traumatic pronouncement came as I sat opposite him at his new headquarters on Sveavagen Street, shortly after the move of the whole operation from Austria.

"When do you want us to start work?" I asked him after briefly chatting about settling into the Swedish way of life.

Earl turned his head and after a brief silence, spoke up. "What do you mean by 'we'. You mean 'when does Laura

145

start work?'" said Earl, not looking up at me as he sat by his desk. "I am afraid we have no work for you, Hannu."

I was dumbstruck. Those few fleeting words had broken my spirit into a thousand pieces. I blinked, wanting to believe that I had not heard correctly his termination announcement.

As I fought back tears of frustration, Earl went on to explain the reason for his decision.

"You see, Hannu, John, my elder son, is returning from America to work with me and he will be taking over your position."

"But you did not mention this when you announced the move here," I weakly tried to protest.

"I am sorry, Hannu," he continued, holding up a placating palm, "but my decision is final!"

Frantic thoughts began to whirl around in my mind. Then I realized that I was to blame in part for this decision. For one, there had been occasions when I had disputed Biblical doctrine.

I could see from Earl's expression, that the conversation was now over. I left the room totally devastated and shocked at the speed with which my world had collapsed around me. As the door closed behind me, I sensed deep in my spirit that this door would never again open up to me.

With a sheet of tears blinding my vision, I stumbled out into the street, followed by my distraught wife who had guessed what had just happened. The summer sun was still shining, but I no longer noticed the beauty of the Swedish summer. Although it was warm, I felt icy cold inside. The birds were merrily singing, but my heart was mourning.

Laura lovingly grasped my hand and tried to console me, but I would not be comforted. She tried to tell me that nothing could happen without God's consent.

"Trust in God," she told me. But I would not listen. I felt deserted, rejected, despised and cast away. It was the lowest point of my life.

We sat down on a park bench just around the corner from the office and, once again, I burst out weeping uncontrollably. There was no end to the flood of tears.

I had come to Europe from Canada to participate in Christian ministry. Now I was without a job in a strange country. I had no acquaintances except for my beloved Laura. As far as I was concerned, I was in my personal "valley of the shadow of death." Total darkness had descended on my soul. I was a foreigner in a foreign land.

For the long, lonely days ahead, I would weep. Laura tried to comfort me, but to no avail. I would not listen. The pain was too hard for me to bear. I hurt so badly on the inside, I would even ask Laura not to speak to me. The wounds were so deep, I began to think that they would never heal.

But Laura's tranquility about what she was convinced was God's sovereign will, started to have an impact on me. She had not shed a tear and her quiet love and compassion for me began to help me to begin to heal.

One day, in my bedroom, I took out a pen and wrote in my diary: "September 17, 1977. Lord, I wait quietly. Your Will be done. Let me not give up in the face of trial. Let me be faithful to Your call in my life. I know that someday Your sun will again shine in my path, my path of total surrender for Russia."

Laura stayed on with Earl Poysti in his radio outreach. There would be occasions that Earl would give me short-term projects on my travels to the USSR. I eventually found my way into a Russian literature ministry in Stockholm.

By now, we had been involved with Poysti's ministry for three years, and I became aware that although we had learned a lot from this great man of God, Laura's time with him was drawing to a close.

Both Laura and I had learned valuable lessons in walking the pathway of faith.

Laura's pay was small and we were completely dependent on the Lord for his provisions for our every need.

I can vividly remember one morning opening the refrigerator, only to find it empty, except for one already opened liter of milk. Payday was still a week away. I was thankful to God that we did not have children at the time. As adults I was also aware that we would somehow survive, and that God did not want to let us go hungry.

Later in that day, I found an unexpected check in the mail from a friend. It was good for a whole month. As I gazed in awe at the check, I recalled the song, "His eye is on the sparrow and I know He watches me!" I knew that our Heavenly Father was watching every step we took.

Shortly after this, Ingemar Martinson, the director of the Slavic Mission in Sweden, spoke words of encouragement to me. He reminded me that God was not subject to "men's actions when His will is in question."

He paused briefly, then went on to tell me. "Hannu, His Will for your life is not in question. God is above human influence. What we think is wrong, God can turn around for the better for us."

Day by day, a feeling of restlessness began also to grow in Laura's heart—as if the nest in Sweden was being dismantled piece by piece. This was hastened by the news that Earl Poysti had decided to transfer his operations to Estes Park, a beautiful mountain city that nestles in the Rocky Mountains of Colorado.

Laura relayed this news to me one evening after returning home from the studio. "There is talk of a possible move of the studio to the USA," she said with a hint of sadness in her voice. "I don't want to leave Europe. In fact, I want to be closer to the Soviet Union."

Instead of heading west, Laura was now setting her sights firmly on the East—possibly Finland.

During a visit to Stockholm, Kai Antturi, a well-known Pentecostal movement leader in Finland and the chairman of the board for IBRA Radio in Finland, heard of our plight. Kai was a long-time friend of Laura's family in the USSR and she had translated for him on numerous occasions during his visits there.

"We don't have any peace about moving to the States," I told Kai, as we met in our home.

He rubbed his chin and then said, "Why don't you come and work with us in Finland? We could initiate a Russian-language cassette ministry with the both of you in charge."

Finland's geopolitical situation with the Soviet Union as its eastern neighbor was sometimes perplexing. There were many unspoken restraints as to what the Finnish government

148

did, both domestically and internationally. The nation's foreign policy was muted and carefully implemented so as not to offend "Big Brother" across the border. The Finnish Press also exercised self-censorship in publishing anything that could be interpreted by the hard men of the Kremlin to be hostile or harmful to Finnish-Soviet relations.

In the media, criticism of the USSR, its foreign policy or even internal affairs, was out of the question.

A NEW AND EXCITING DOOR

In June of 1980, after much prayer, we packed our few belongings and headed by ferry to Helsinki, convinced that God had opened up a new and exciting door for us to walk through. IBRA Radio Finland, had been established in 1955 as an alternative to government-controlled radio and television, but still they were not allowed to broadcast internally because that was all state controlled. This Scandinavian Christian ministry supported Christian radio in countries like Japan, Kenya, Thailand and Uruguay. The USSR, however, was top priority for IBRA. The latter's programming was supplied by Earl Poysti, as IBRA Finland had no local production in the Russian language. To join IBRA Finland was definitely a step of faith for Laura and me as they had no full-time staff, no Russian program production and an ever-shrinking budget.

The move to Finland also meant for us having to adjust to a new situation. After working with Earl Poysti's excellent facilities, all we had now was an old Studer tape recorder housed in the recording studio of R.V. Publishers, the same the Christian publishing house where I had worked some four years earlier. IBRA Radio had just enough resources to pay Laura a wage for initially translating selected sermons and Bible courses into Russian and then reading them onto audio cassette that would then be smuggled into the Soviet Union. I was told that I would have to work on a volunteer basis.

Some members of the IBRA board of directors were family friends with Earl and consequently they showed a cautious attitude toward me. They were aware of my problems with Earl. I found this situation to be emotionally depressing.

THE ULTIMATE EMPLOYER

I tried to deal with this feeling of rejection by telling myself that God was my ultimate employer. I prayed that these men would one day see that God had truly called me to this ministry and had given me His vision. I knew that His recommendation was the best that anyone could have.

We settled in Katinala, a small village outside of Helsinki, with a population of about 2,000 people. We were provided a two-bedroom apartment and shown our new accommodation by Heikki and Vilho, two board members who were well-known pastors of churches in their denomination.

They informed us that we would be responsible for a weekly Finnish radio program.

"I am afraid that Russian productions are out of the question for the time being," one of them solemnly announced.

I felt a check in my spirit as I heard this news. My thoughts were far away from Finnish radio amateurs who would hear our broadcasts.

I was not satisfied. Still, I was aware of the Finnish speaking minorities in Russia, Karelia, the Inkeri people who dotted the USSR, and those people who spoke Finnish in Estonia. I knew that they, too, would be listening silently across the border. I found comfort in at least being able to minister to them.

Laura and I looked around the spartan apartment. I asked the board members where the studio and equipment were. The men eyed each other, smiling cynically.

"Well, there is a spare bedroom over there," said Heikki finally. "Maybe you could take a tape recorder, close the door, and record the programs in there."

I looked toward the door and forced a smile. I was glad that God had given me enough foresight to ask my home church in Vancouver, a few months earlier, to grant me the funds to purchase a small tape recorder, a mixer and a microphone. Two of my childhood friends, Merja Koivumäki and Jouko Noso, gave considerable donations out of their personal funds for this equipment.

150

My heart yearned for Laura and I to minister to Russians in their native tongue, but the board were still far from accepting that idea. To an extent, I understood their rationale as the politics and geography of Finland had also influenced much of the thinking inside the church. To many Finnish Christians, the Soviet Union was a terrifying, closed, Communist-controlled state that could attack their homeland like a coiled rattlesnake, at any time. The threat of its deadly venom was enough to deter many Finnish people from doing anything that would upset the Soviets.

"Lord," I prayed one day as Laura kneeled beside me in our bedroom after we had read the Scriptures, "please open the door to us for ministry in the Russian language." It made all the sense in the world because practically all of the 290 million people living in the USSR spoke Russian.

Had heaven heard my prayer? I didn't know. I hadn't heard any voices or seen any visions. But there was a conviction deep in my heart that God would respond in His own time.

Meanwhile, the two of us busied ourselves in producing radio programs for the Finnish minorities in the USSR, most of whom lived close to the Finnish frontier.

I found it difficult to produce these Finnish programs in the primitive conditions of our spare room, so I seized a hammer and saw and started to build a control room and recording booth in the bedroom.

As I toiled, I prayed, "Lord, let this humble structure serve the Russian people as well in the days to come. God, please open up the hearts of the board members to see that the harvest is so much more plentiful, that You will bless us financially to cover the costs involved."

Laura also quietly prayed about the situation, but she was also a realist about the situation. She knew that I did not yet speak Russian well enough to be a radio preacher. So she set about helping me study the language.

A breakthrough in our dream of ministering to the USSR finally came in the fall of 1981, when Jack Koziol, the veteran director of the Russian department of Far Eastern Broadcasting Company, visited Finland along with his wife, Vera.

I had gone to a service in a Helsinki church, thinking that I was to meet another Russian-language broadcaster. Jack, who had served FEBC for decades, happened to be the guest speaker at that afternoon meeting. After he had completed his presentation, I engaged him in conversation. Jack recognized me as a former employee of Earl Poysti's ministry, and asked me how I was faring and what I was doing.

"I'm doing a Finnish program on shortwave," replied.

Jack looked puzzled. "You mean to say that you are doing nothing in Russian," he said. "You were in production with Earl, weren't you?"

"Yes," I replied.

"Then, why are you not doing anything in Russian now?" Clearly, he was driving at something.

"Well," I stammered, "it is because our Finnish sponsors have said there is no money available for Russian language transmissions."

I knew that Laura would have said that it was also because I did not speak Russian well enough.

THE PROPOSAL

Without hesitation, Jack said, "If you can produce a weekly program in Russian, we will air it on all of our stations at no charge to you."

I could hardly contain my excitement, as I saw Jack's promise as the fulfillment of my prayers. Also, I now realized that God does not make mistakes.

Jack explained that the Far Eastern Broadcast Company broadcast from transmitters in the Philippines, South Korea and Redwood City in California. (They later added a transmitter on Saipan Island in the South Pacific.)

I could hardly contain myself as I listened to this dramatic proposal. We could go on the air in Russian, not over one station, but four. And we did not need any money to do this. This news was too good to be true. I was suddenly jubilant. Something sprang to life inside of me. I could scarcely believe the offer that Jack had just made.

"Yes, we'll produce the program," I finally stated.

"Send us a pilot program and we will listen to it, and, if it meets our requirements, we will put it on the air," he told me as he smiled gently.

Shortly afterwards, I met with Heikki and Vilho, but their reaction to the news was muted.

Finally, Heikki responded. "We will wait to see what happens," he declared.

Still, the full board cautiously accepted our plans, especially when they learned that there would be no added expense. It was tough for some of them as they voiced their fear of the political repercussions in Finland to Russian language production.

The concern of the Finnish brethren turned out to be somewhat warranted. After we began to prepare programming for the broadcasts, the Communist party of Finland suddenly developed a peculiar sense of concern for the "spiritual welfare" of the people of its eastern neighbor.

Laura and I had decided to produce an interview-type program where interesting people would talk about the mighty works of God in their lives. We settled on a format of interviews with Christian leaders and missionaries in the fifteen-minute weekly production. The name was to be "Dateline," or "Aktualno/Nasushono" in Russian.

Laura was to be chief producer and she also proofread all my scripts. Most importantly, she would help record my portions in the Russian language. She turned out to be a hard taskmaster and, at times, would reduce me to tears with her tutoring. If my pronunciation was not good enough, she would stop me after every second word, if necessary.

"A more pronounced G or B or D please, Hannu," she would insist as I would keep on trying to meet her high standards. I would often have to do the script twenty times and still she would not be satisfied.

"DEATH TO THE PIGS"

We had not yet broadcast a single program when a headline appeared in the Communist press that lambasted us. It read: "DEATH TO THE PIGS! THE REVOLUTION IS UN-

DER WAY! SUNDAY EVENING OPIUM TO THE SOVIET UNION!"

The hair-raising article pulled no punches and was obviously designed to whip up negative feelings against us. As expected, the story caught the attention of SUPO, the Finnish Intelligence Agency. Acting upon orders from the Foreign Ministry, two agents from the Tampere Division, made an unannounced visit to our "revolutionary headquarters."

The plainclothed officers were friendly and apologetic. They explained to me that they had been sent to investigate the truth of the article.

"Can we hear some samples of your programs?" one of them asked.

"Sure," I replied as I took a spool of tape and wound it on a machine.

After listening to this and other programs, and then checking our equipment, they decided that everything was in order.

"You may continue with your activities," said one of the intelligence officers. "You have our consent to go ahead."

Not long after this visit, an apology that confessed to spreading false information mysteriously appeared in the same newspaper. It read: "The newspaper regrets the erroneous facts published in an article on the radio work of IBRA Finland. The correct facts are as follows..." What followed was a statement about the scope of our programming for an international audience. They made it clear that the programs were to be transmitted over a commercial station in Portugal and pointed out that there was "no clandestine transmitter in Finland" that was broadcasting this message to the USSR.

Surprisingly, the Finnish Security Police had requested that the paper run an article correcting the facts in the article published earlier.

September 5, 1981 was an historic day for me. It was the day that my dreams were to finally come true. At 20:45 Moscow time, the first Russian program produced in our bedroom studio, was due to hit the airwaves. This particular one was a pilot that carried a ten-minute apologetic message from me on the existence of God. I mentioned that famous scientists like Blaise Pascal, Isaac Newton and Louis Pasteur, all had a deep faith in God.

Its broadcast coincided with an evening service I was due to attend in Helsinki. At the prescribed hour, I carried my little shortwave transistor radio outside the building and stood outside under a starry night sky, to hear the identifying fanfare introducing the program.

Though it was coming in from Lisbon, Portugal, 1,500 miles away, the reception was crystal clear. As I listened to the program, I had no trouble envisaging the radio waves blanketing all of the western USSR at that very moment, penetrating the walls of homes right across that region.

I closed my eyes and visualized the looks on people's faces as they listened to the Gospel, some fascinated, others crying, others bewildered, still others questioning the purpose of life. Potentially, millions would be hearing this same broadcast.

I was overwhelmed. I looked up at the stars above and remembered Abraham and how God had faithfully fulfilled His promise to him. That despite the odds, the delays, and the resistance, the God of Abraham had brought it to pass. He was also MY GOD! My vision had, at last, taken to the sky!

Chapter Twenty-One

From The Moon To Russia

Few people in all of Soviet history have been worshipped as much as Yuri Alekseyevich Gagarin, who first entered our "Good Ship Earth" in 1931.

It was some thirty years later, that, after rigorous training, his big day finally arrived. It was April 12, 1961, when Gagarin battled "G" forces on board the single-earth orbit flight of the Soviet Union's Vostok 1 spacecraft. That event is regarded as man's first true space flight. Five more flights of the Vostok spacecraft were to follow.

Upon his return from orbit, Gagarin had proclaimed, "There is no God!" Whether these words had been coined by himself or his country's ideologues, I don't know, but they certainly earned him a place in the Soviet Union's "Hall of Fame." Those four words became symbolic of Soviet atheistic ideology. Every student and child in the country now knew by heart "Uncle Yuri's" declaration of unbelief.

According to official sources, Yuri died in a plane crash while on a training flight. There is another version of his death, however, which is not so valiant. Sources within the USSR claim that his plane never crashed, but apparently Gagarin lived for sixteen years after he was officially buried in 1984.

SPACE ODDITY

In 1981, an article appeared in the local newspaper of Gagarin's home town of Kaluga. According to this story, Gagarin had been sent to a psychiatric hospital following a blazing row with Chairman Leonid Brezhnev at a drinking party in the Kremlin. Reportedly, the cosmonaut got into a verbal argument with Brezhnev. Drunk and raging, Gagarin tossed a glass of wine into the Chairman's red rosy face.

"You will regret this," railed Brezhnev, who was beside himself with rage.

Yuri Gagarin was sent to a psychiatric hospital from which he briefly escaped. The spaceman had arrived at his home and pounded on the door, begging his mother to "open up." She never did, believing Yuri was dead and fearing a trick by local hoodlums.

Years later, after being told that her son had lived long after the plane crash report, Gagarin's mother suffered a nervous breakdown. She had recognized his voice from behind the door as that of her son. Horrified that she had turned him away, it had been too much for her.

* * * * *

In August of 1971, an American spacecraft, Apollo 15, had roared into outer space. Its destination was the moon. On board were three Americans: Al Worden, Dave Scott and James B. Irwin. Two of them descended to the moon's surface.

According to Irwin, out of twenty-four astronauts that actually flew on the Apollo missions, only three were confessing atheists. The rest professed to believe in the existence of a supernatural God, a creator.

I had met Colonel Irwin for the first time in Colorado Springs, just months before I had married Laura. I was on assignment in America doing some interviews for a Finnish monthly magazine. His conversation was one in a series I was conducting.

Colonel Irwin's inspiring story about his faith in God was in total conflict with that of Yuri Gagarin.

SPIRITUAL DARKNESS

Raimo Grönroos, my friend who had counseled me on the day I had proposed to Laura, and Donald Best, the owner of the Best Locks Corporation in Indianapolis, Indiana, were at that time working on a proposed visit by Jim Irwin to the USSR. I was invited to assist Raimo, who like me had considerable experience in traveling there. The prospect of joining Colonel Irwin on a trip to the Soviet Union was a dream. It sounded like a fabulous missionary journey to a country that Irwin believed to be in spiritual darkness. Obviously, I wanted to go!

There was one drawback, however. What would the authorities say about Irwin's visit and what would be the repercussions for me? I was already teetering on the verge of exile. If the excursion turned out to be a powerful blessing, chances were it would be my last trip to Russia. I calculated that for the authorities it would probably be the last drop.

I frantically turned the issue over in my mind, weighing the pros and cons. Finally, I decided I would go! I knew that multitudes in the Soviet Union would be touched by the astronaut's testimony.

The departure date came almost too fast. There was no turning back. With us for that historic journey were Jim and Mary Irwin, and six other Americans.

Jim Irwin had accepted an invitation from Bondarenko to come to Russia. Intourist, the only authorized institution for looking after tourists in the Soviet Union, handled all hotel reservations and travel between cities. Beyond a doubt, the Apollo astronaut was a VIP for Intourist—possibly the first astronaut to be given such a broad itinerary in the Soviet Union.

Bondarenko, on the other hand had taken care of coordinating all of the church activity on the trip. Intourist, and the KGB for that matter, had no idea of Jim Irwin's intentions of meeting with Soviet believers.But they were taking no chances. Bondarenko was now under arrest in solitary confinement in the city of Krasnodar because of his arrangements. Joseph was interrogated for months afterwards without any charges being leveled against him.

Bondarenko had done a thorough job arranging Irwin's itinerary. The journey was to include visits to churches in the cities of Tallinn, Riga, Kiev, Odessa, Charkov and Moscow.

Our ten-member delegation passed through customs with relative ease. Mary and Jim Irwin's twelve suitcases were not even opened. Customs seemed to be keenly aware of the astronaut's arrival. Nonetheless Donald Best and I were subjected to a closer screening. One inspecting officer pulled out a Russian translation of my published interview with Colonel Irwin. He lay my belongings aside and started to read the interview. Engulfed in the text, he soaked in every word.

"Is the astronaut with you?" he asked and continued reading. A half hour slipped by. Suddenly a high ranking officer appeared, putting the rest of the inspection into high gear.

"The astronaut himself is waiting in the lounge!"

Another officer came up to the counter where I stood. "Is there really an astronaut at customs?"

A moment later we were given a green light. Don and I repacked our bags and strode out to meet the others. It was five thirty in the afternoon by the time we arrived at Hotel Viru. A Volga with four plain clothes police followed us to the hotel.

"State Security", I thought, "This time they had a valid reason to keep watch over us".

We checked in and scuttled off to St. Olav's church for the seven o'clock service. St. Olav's Church was built in the year 1260 by the Roman Catholics. Its steeple rose to a height of 365 feet above the city. It was visible from international waters in the Gulf of Finland. Later, it was used as a German Lutheran Church. After the Second World War, the government surrendered it to the so-called evangelical denominations and it was now being used by the Baptist/Pentecosal congregation affiliated with the Moscow Baptist Union and had about 1500 members. The inside appearance of the main sanctuary, which was rectangular in shape, was that of a central European cathedral.

The building was made of stone and chandeliers hung from the ceiling. It had a balcony for the choir along the back of the sanctuary. The massive pipe organ, the largest in Europe until 1978, was also located in the balcony.

Seating was on the ground level and there was a large platform for guests and clergy to sit on.

Oddly, confirmation of the exact day of Jim Irwin's arrival had not reached the church leadership. Since it was a midweek service and prayer meeting night the main sanctuary was only half full. Someone quickly slipped word to the elders and pastors that the astronaut had entered the building. The pastors took immediate action. Messengers were dispatched throughout the city — some traveling by car, some by foot. Others manned telephones.

Meantime, in the service, one of the pastors bargained for time. He asked each member of our group to prepare a short greeting. The congregation sang hymns like "How Great Thou Art," in the Estonian language. The astronaut would not be speaking until the end of the service. Soon people started to flow into the building.

Finally Pastor Merilo was satisfied. Every seat in the sanctuary was full and hundreds of people were standing in the aisle, balconies and along the back wall. It was record-breaking attendance for St. Olav's Church. Pastor Merilo was assisted by Dr. Tark, a scholar and graduate of the theological department of Columbia University in the USA.

Jim Irwin stood up and ascended to the pulpit which was perched some fifteen feet above the assembly. No pastor in all of Russia would ever have dared dream that a person of such stature would enter its doors, never mind speak to the people. And, even more bizarre, the guest was a professing Christian — a man who believed that Jesus Christ was the Son of God.

"I bring you greetings from the moon and from America!" Jim started. Everyone in the auditorium seemed to hold their breath. Before them was a man who had surpassed the achievements of the Soviet cosmonauts. This man had walked on the moon. No Soviet had ever done that. Every Soviet cosmonaut was a superhero. This man was an even greater a superhero. Jim proceeded to talk about the existence of God from the biblical and scientific viewpoints. He related how he had found a meaningful faith in God, how he had experienced God's presence and help on the moon flight. I could see many people all over the auditorium in tears, others with smiles of deep satisfaction. It was as if they were saying: "We knew our scientists weren't telling the whole truth! Yuri Gagarin where are you now? You ought to hear this!"

The three-hour service was over but people were not about to go home. A few brave ones lunged forward towards the astronaut. Then the whole audience, catching on, surged toward the podium like an incoming tide. Soon Jim and Mary Irwin were totally encompassed by an uncontrollable mass of autograph-hungry people. Those coming in from behind were pressing those standing before them. Inside the wall of human flesh Raimo and I tried to keep the astronaut from being crushed. We shouted commands, but no one was listening. Everyone was hysterically trying to push a piece of paper, a card, a book, a New Testament to Jim and Mary for their signature.

It was fifteen after ten at night and the people were still in church. Finally the pastor announced that only young people could stay behind as the astronaut would be talking to them in the adjacent side chapel. Three hundred students and young people squeezed into the room. Jim showed slides from the moon flight and fielded questions that his audience tirelessly pitched during the additional ninety minutes.

The questions indicated that Soviet atheistic ideology had done a poor job in erasing religion from the hearts of these young people. If Yuri Gagarin was right then these young people weren't prepared to accept his statement at face value. Their souls ached for answers to questions about their origin and purpose. It was impossible to reconcile the differing views on the origin of the universe as advocated by the Soviet and American space programs.

Neil Armstrong, the first human to walk on the moon, had read from Genesis 1:1 "In the beginning God created the heavens and the earth". Whether Armstrong personally believed it was a another matter. What was clear was that there were many others, responsible for taking Armstrong to the moon who did believe it. Dr. Werner Von Braun, the mastermind behind the whole Apollo program was one.

Irwin then made an altar call and some fifteen young people came forward to commit their lives to Jesus Christ.

Before leaving, he presented the church with a framed picture of himself in a spacesuit, standing on the moon saluting the American flag. He scribbled on the corner of the picture, "God walking on the earth is more important than man walking on the moon."

It was midnight by the time we all finally said good night to our Soviet hosts. Jim and Mary had received a beautiful bouquet of roses, which was a custom at that time in the Soviet Union. The rest of us received carnations.

A lot of things pointed to the fact that State Security, quietly working with Intourist, wanted to make a favorable impression on the astronaut. Donald, Jim's closest aide, found an issue of The Moscow News in the English language in his hotel room. The issue just happened to have a big article on the Soviet space program.

Despite the late hour I decided to run down to the telegraph office to call my wife in Stockholm. The weather was beautiful and warm. We talked for about five minutes. There was no one on the streets at that time of night except a couple of shadows. Stepping out of the telegraph office I noticed three men following me. Amused, I stopped to say hello.

"Nice night, great time to be out for a breath of fresh air!" explained the trio.

I looked at my watch. One thirty in the morning! The streets were deserted except for myself and my buddies! We had all developed a craving for fresh air at the same time, and strangely, the same place.

The next day we boarded a JAK 40 jet aircraft. The JAK 40 resembles the American McDonnell Douglas DC-9 except that they are considerably shorter. As the aircraft touched down in Riga, Joseph's home city, after the short one-hour flight, I wondered what would happen. The authorities must have been wary about Joseph's "mysterious" absence. I almost expected them to release Joseph for the duration of the astronaut's visit but they did not.

Security at Riga airport was tight and no one was allowed to come near us. The reception party of local believers stood behind erected barriers no closer that fifty yards away. Joseph was not in their midst.

We had lunch at the Hotel Riga. The director of Intourist arranged for a small reception and asked Jim for his autograph. This was ironic as these same people had always been hostile to Western believers wishing to fellowship with their brethren here.

This trip was no exception. Coordination of all contacts between our group and Russian believers was my primary responsibility. I had called Andrey Bondarenko (Joseph's nephew, also a brilliant evangelist) and checked the evening's itinerary. On his way to meet us at the hotel Andrey had stopped by his church to take care of some business. On his way out of the compound he found the gate locked. Someone had locked the only entrance to the church while he was inside. There was no other way out.

St. Matthew's Church, a large cathedral, built before Communist rule, was a registered or "legal" Latvian Pentecostal Church. A legal church had consented to the conditions for worship set forth by KGB. The very idea that worship was regulated by the KGB was a contradiction. Worshippers were not as aware of all the compromise involved as the church leadership were. Many a pastor had sold his loyalty to the state. God's Word was subject to approval by men.

Those who chose not to compromise were destined to walk the way of Joseph and multitudes of others like him.

We were on time. And St. Matthew's was full to overflowing. Jim decided again to make an altar call. Many in that service raised their hands, indicating that they wanted to make a decision for Christ that afternoon. He then asked them to come forward and local members of the church provided the counseling.

We were then whisked off right after the meeting, to meet with various local Christian leaders who provided a wonderful spread of food for us to enjoy.

Jim was to hold a press conference in the hotel the following day. APN (Agenstvo Press Novostyay), the largest news agency in the Soviet Union, wanted to chat with this rare guest.

Under the direction of Alexander Yemelyanov, the news bureau chief in Latvia, who was dressed in a light brown suit, white shirt and matching striped tie, three journalists showed up. Jim answered questions on the moon flight and the space program. I was impressed at how intimately Jim was aware of practically all his colleagues' whereabouts and present occupations. There were over twenty of them.

Our second service was to be held in a four-room apartment suite in the center of the city—under the disguise of a birthday party. It was Joseph's home church. The church was one of the so-called underground churches of Russia. We had not wanted to influence the planning of the itinerary in any way, leaving it totally in the hands of Joseph and his aides.

On the way to "church" we stopped by a bakery to pick up a delicious looking cream cake. The place was jam packed. I estimated about two hundred people to be present. The "birthday party" went well until halfway through Jim's presentation. Then I noticed people getting restless by the main entrance. Suspecting that something was wrong I got up on my chair for a better look. I could see a number of police hats with their distinct red bands.

The police had arrived to break up the underground service. It was apparent that they had no knowledge of the astronaut's presence. I clicked a few pictures with my Nikon and sat down. Jim bowed toward me and asked what was going on.

"The police have arrived!" I said.

"I see", said Jim and continued preaching as if nothing had happened. Now I understood why Jim had been chosen as an astronaut. He did not react to difficult circumstances negatively.

Mary, Jim's wife wasn't quite as cool as her husband.

"What's up?" whispered Mary who was sitting on my other side.

"The police have come. It looks like they're going to break up the service," I said. "Oh no! What are we going to do now?" Mary was panicking.

"Nothing" I said. That was a pretty exhaustive answer.

It didn't take long for the police to catch on that international guests were present. In the middle of the commotion one officer picked up a few words of Jim's speech.

"What! Are there foreigners in this place?" asked an officer. By this time the other law enforcement officers had also stopped what they were doing.

"Oh yes", volunteered a believer.

"Who"?

"Astronaut James Irwin from Apollo 15, you know the one who has walked on the moon", said another, almost boasting. That was enough for the police.

"We're going for reinforcements," said one of the police as they strode out of the apartment. A while later three higher ranking officers returned, this time very quietly, very politely. They led the owner of the apartment to a side room for a soft rebuke.

"Don't you know that inviting such high level international guests into private homes is not allowed in our country!" said the lawman. "You will promise to never do this again!" he added.

"I promise", said the man of the house, a small smile at the corners of his mouth.

The officers left. And the service continued without further interruption.

The authorities had managed to successfully embarrass themselves by demonstrating to foreign guests how the much publicized freedom of religion worked in Soviet society.

Apollo 15 astronaut James Irwin on tour in Russia. After this trip Hannu was exiled for eleven years.

Chapter Twenty-Two

Prisoners Of Conscience

Kiev, the Capital of the Soviet republic of Ukraine was the next stop on our agenda. Known as the "mother of Russian cities," Ancient Kiev was now capital of the Ukrainian Soviet Socialist Republic, by far the largest and most important of the republics after Russia proper. Situated on the banks of the Dnepr River, just below its confluence with the Desna River, Kiev a city of about 2.2 million is a major port and was one of the largest and most important cities of the Soviet Union.

Irwin visited the autonomously registered Baptist church, formerly under the pastorate of Georgi Vins—the charismatic leader of the underground Baptist movement. Vins was not there because he too was in prison serving a long sentence. After Vins was taken away the church leadership decided to register autonomously. This meant that the church had not

167

accepted the terms for registration that were usually required. This type of registration was not available in the early 1960s when the church was forced underground following a new crackdown by the authorities on church activity. In the few cases where churches were autonomously registered much depended upon the goodwill of local authorities.

In each city, surveillance of our group's movements got tighter as we progressed. The authorities were catching on. The main purpose of Astronaut Irwin's trip was not to see the USSR but to visit Christians in every city. To their disgust it went even further. Irwin was out to preach the Gospel in every city.

Our next stop was Odessa, the famed Black Sea port, which was the administrative, industrial and cultural center of Odessa Oblast, Ukraine Soviet Socialist Republic.

Odessa, which was one of the largest ports in the Soviet Union, was important strategically to the Soviet military, but also has plenty of attraction for Western as well as domestic tourists. The city is also a spa and vacation resort, known for its twenty-five miles of sandy beaches and its therapeutic mud baths and sanitariums.

A well-planned and handsome city, Odessa's streets and boulevards are laid out in regular, tree-lined blocks. The Potemkin Steps descend from a square in the city center to Odessa Bay. The city is home to a number of museums, an observatory, a conservatory, concert halls, libraries, and a motion picture studio.

Our first service was held in the registered Baptist church. The official name of the church is the All Union Council Of Evangelical Christians and Baptists Church in Odessa. It was comprised of not only Baptists but Pentecostals as well. An unlikely union but very real nonetheless, in the USSR. The reason was that in 1962 when the council was officially formed, Pentecostals as well as other Protestant churches were not allowed to register under their own identity. The government wanted everything under one lid.

For the first time I noticed that Soviet military personnel were present at one of our meetings. At the far end of the sanctuary up on the balcony sat two men in blue uniforms. I went up to the balcony for a good shot of the crowd below.

This put me in range of the two men. As I walked by them I recognized their markings. They were Soviet air force officers. The sight of the Soviet military in Protestant meetings was uncommon. There was no future in the military for religious people. It was obvious that these individuals had come on assignment from headquarters. They paid undivided attention to what the American astronaut was saying. To them Irwin had special significance.

The next service in Odessa was held in another autonomously registered church. Irwin had suffered a heart attack after his moon flight and was now showing signs of fatigue. The journey had been compact, fast moving and busy. Believers in every city wanted to make the most of this prestigious visit. Right after his speech Jim motioned to me that it was time to take him directly to the hotel.

The pastor volunteered to drive us to the hotel in his red Moskvitch automobile. Jim then handed Vasily a stack of enlarged, four-color, autographed pictures of the moon and a number of business cards with John 3:16 in Russian, printed on the back.

It was already dark. As we got in the car I noticed that something was happening about fifty feet away. Car doors started to slam. As we drove by the spot the head lamps of a Volga switched on as the vehicle fell in line behind us.

On the way to the hotel Jim surrendered the promised souvenirs to Vasily. Just around the corner from the hotel Jim and I disembarked. Vasily and the pastor continued on. We later found out that a minute later they had been stopped and arrested by the police. Vasily had been interrogated all night and his precious souvenirs had been confiscated.

The authorities had reason for concern. The Soviet Union was supposed to be an atheistic society. Suddenly here was a man whose personal or professional achievements far surpassed those of Soviet spacemen. Cosmonauts were little gods. Irwin not only believed in God but was actively encouraging others to do the same.

It was starting to dawn on me that someone would be held responsible for the cumulative result of Astronaut Irwin's missionary trip to Russia. There were only two men in the group who could be considered as administrative directors on the tour. Administrative directors made perfect scapegoats. One was my friend Raimo, who without warning decided to leave the group in Odessa and return to Helsinki. There were still two cities to go before the trip was over. I suspected Raimo sensed imminent trouble and sought to steer clear of a clash with authorities. Moscow would be the place for the final showdown.

It is said that in Soviet Ukraine all roads lead to Khar'kov. From its early days as a fort in the 17th century down through World War II, Khar'kov had been repeatedly ravaged by war. Each time a new city was erected. In World War II it was seized by the Germans and some 100,000 citizens died during the occupation. The battle to free it in 1943 destroyed half of its buildings.

Our roads certainly led us to this agricultural trading center also known as the "Pittsburgh of Russia. "

The big difference between the two cities was religious freedom. Two weeks before our arrival in the city, the KGB had carried out a "mop-up" operation in the local churches. Twenty-five brothers had been arrested in one church alone. The night before our arrival four more had been taken away. So it was no surprise that a group of believers in one of the biggest services of our trip hoisted up a banner bearing the poignant words, "Remember the prisoners." Government agents who were present in the meeting, soon moved into the crowd and tore down the sign. In another development, my room was searched in my absence. When I found that it had been ransacked, I complained to the hotel director.

"Mr. Haukka," he said with a tone of indifference in his voice, "I think the authorities were justified as you are not a regular tourist."

Still, despite the dramas we had experienced at the hands of the KGB, the group enjoyed the trip immensely, Jim perhaps the most. Thousands of Soviets had turned out to hear his powerful testimony. He had conquered the hearts of Russian believers who desperately needed the reinforcement his words of faith had given them. They had responded to the "space traveler" by pouring out their love and respect for him. Young people in every city had come forward to express their faith in Jesus Christ.

The irritation of the authorities had grown steadily as we went from city to city. Even with Joseph Bondarenko behind bars, the authorities seemed to think that things had gone far too smoothly. Coordination inside the group was hard for them to hinder.

We were in for a mild surprise upon our arrival in Moscow. The Intourist guide met us at the airport and stated that the group would reside at the Hotel Rossia.

"You," she said pointed a finger in my face, "will need to stay at the Hotel Metropol." Obviously, I was considered to be the main troublemaker of the group, and so I would be separated from them.

I was aware that the Hotel Rossia was at that time the world's largest hotel and located right on the edge of Red Square, the very heart of the "Evil Empire."

She smiled maliciously as she added, "There is just no room for you at that hotel."

Alarm bells went off in my head. I could not and would not stay alone in a different hotel. I had heard many wild stories about westerners being drugged, harassed, and visited at night and set up with false charges.

"I will not stay at the Hotel Metropol," I insisted, standing my ground.

"I am sorry, Mr. Haukka," she went on, "but these are my instructions."

I traveled with the group to the Hotel Rossia and went to the reception desk. I wanted to check out the situation for myself.

"Are there any vacancies?" I asked the woman behind the desk.

She opened up a large reservations book and started to shuffle the pages of vacant room numbers. "We have vacancies. Which room would you like?"

My face lit up like a lamp. I was visibly relieved.

At that moment, our guide interrupted the proceedings. "The reception," she snapped angrily, "does not have the authority to decide where you will be staying. We will have to call the general director of Intourist."

With that, she leaned over the counter and picked up a phone and began dialing a series of numbers. I understood him to say in Russian, "Boris Vasilievitch, I am calling regarding Haukka."

Comrade Vasilievitch obviously cut into her words and I overheard him say that I had to go into the other hotel.

"But, Boris Vasilievitch, there is room in the hotel ..."

This brought a response that was so loud that I could hear it even clearer from ten feet away.

"Tell Haukka that there is no room for him at the Hotel Rossia!"

She slammed down the receiver in the cradle of the phone. She stood and faced me, her face by now blood red. There was nothing to explain. I got the picture.

The KGB had finally deduced that the eight-member American delegation was being escorted by two Finns (Raimo had now returned to Helsinki). They had decided that I had to be separated from the group and that no more protests by me would be tolerated.

The others settled into the Hotel Rossia, and I was told to go to the Hotel Metropol, with a promise that a pass would be issued to me that would allow me to enter the Rossia. The Intourist strategy was well thought out, but they mistakenly believed that they would relieve my anxiety with a piece of paper.

The evening service was fast approaching. I needed to get back with the group. I picked up my pass from the bureau outside the Hotel Metropol and walked back to the Hotel Rossia.

The bouncers at the entrance had apparently been told to watch out for me. At that time, westerners were not usually asked to produce a hotel ID. But the moment I set foot inside the lobby, I was stopped and requested to produce a hotel card or pass. I had the necessary pass and held it up for inspection.

The door man glanced at my pass and promptly tore it up into minute pieces, his face bearing a malevolent grin. "You don't live here and so you won't be needing this," he hissed.

He then grabbed me by the arm and began to haul me out the door. Just then, out of the elevator and into the lobby,

172

stepped Donald Best, our tour's financial manager. The timing was divine. He rushed over towards me and yelled at the man to let me go. With that, the uniformed bellman released his hold on me.

Moscow was to be Jim Irwin's last stop on his tour of the Soviet Union. His first night there saw him traveling with all of us on Moscow's famed subway with its glittering chandeliers, to attend a small meeting in a believer's home.

"There, we discussed their general situation and particular plight, because several brothers were facing prison sentences," said Irwin in a later report. "The brothers said I should try to keep the door open for a return visit." For this opportunity, they recommended that I officially say something good about the Soviet Union and something bad about the Carter administration."

James Irwin had come at the invitation of Joseph Bondarenko, a person he had not seen on his trip. Irwin had been briefed on the situation. To the American, the thought of this man being imprisoned was detestable.

So, when he was granted a visit to the office of Mr. Kuroyedov, the Minister of Religion in the USSR, he decided to seize the opportunity. This man headed up The Council of Religious Affairs of the USSR, whose office was accountable to the atheistic government for all religious activity in the country. Its function was supposedly to ensure the various religious groups with the country the right to worship. Judging by the fruits of its labor, the ministry actually did the opposite, doing all it could to counter the activities of Christians.

The minister was conveniently "not in" when he arrived at the office. His deputy received the American spaceman.

Not wanting to beat about the bush, Jim Irwin told the man, "I have come to the Soviet Union upon the invitation of a pastor named Joseph Bondarenko," he started in. "I have now been in the country for over a week and still have not met my host. Can you please tell me where he is?"

It was a loaded question and the deputy chief was not pleased to hear it. After a long silence, he responded.

"I am amazed that a man of your stature and position, has accepted an invitation to visit our country from a criminal," he said harshly.

Usually a patient man, James Irwin was not having any of this. But he changed his tack of questioning.

"Mr. Deputy Minister," he said as a glint came into his eyes, "please tell me if you personally believe in God or not?"

The official paused briefly, and then said, "Long ago, Colonel Irwin, I used to believe in God. But now I believe only in Lenin and Marx."

Jim Irwin, who had been sitting down across from the Deputy Minister, stood up and said, "Thank you. We have nothing more to discuss."

The visit was over and Jim left the office.

The evening service was a never-to-be forgotten experience. The Central Baptist Church of Moscow was full to overflowing. Students from the prestigious Moscow State University had come out for the service. The service spilled over into a special youth service held in the side sanctuary. Jim had his visual materials and thoroughly enjoyed the challenge of meeting head on with these budding Russian academics. The issue of God plagued these young students. They absorbed every word, expression and reaction of the man from the moon. Only heaven knows what impact the astronaut's testimony would have on these people.

"Church services in Russia are long," wrote Irwin after he returned to the States. "I guess that may be because the believers don't know if they will be able to come together again. Each service was normally four hours [long] and when Mary spoke, the service went on for six hours. "Before the visit, I thought I could never endure such long services, but we found the time flew by."

At the end of this service, as with all of the others, the congregation stood up and slowly waved their hands and sang, "May God be with you till we meet again."

Said Irwin: "I will never forget those haunting, tear-stained faces, the music and the love."

Our return to the hotel presented yet another problem. My pass had been confiscated and torn up by the doorman earlier in the day. I had no intention of parting with my friends.

174

A contact at the Canadian Embassy in Moscow had warned me against spending the night alone.

"Don't worry," said Jim as I approached the main entrance with a trace of anxiety. "Let me go first and then you follow directly behind me. Don Best will be third. OK?"

It sounded fine to me. Jim's slight frame led the way and stepped into the lobby. I was next. As soon as he saw me, the doorman sprang to life. Stepping toward me, he latched onto my left bicep and proceeded to pull me in the direction of the door.

Don was already inside the lobby, standing dead in his tracks. Jim turned around. Without a moment's hesitation, he ran up and grabbed me by my other arm. It was a tug-of-war! The bouncer was pulling on one end and Jim on the other. The spectacle was stopped by a shout from down the hall. It was the supervisor for hotel security.

"Let go of him," he yelled in Russian. "It's the astronaut on the other end." The bouncer let go immediately.

Despite the debacle, I spent the night safely with my group at the hotel.

"These Russian Christians asked that I take their greetings back to you," wrote Irwin. "We saw their restrictions and persecution firsthand, so we know they are hurting."

"They pointed out that when one part of the Body of Christ is hurting, the whole body is hurting. We hear a great deal about the Jewish dissidents, but we rarely hear about our Russian believers who face trials every day."

He added, "Our Christian lives will never be the same, because we were with our Russian brothers and sisters. They took us into their churches, their homes and their hearts. New friendships were formed halfway around the world. They are a most generous people with their food, gifts and fellowship."

"A Russian believer is one who has made a deep commitment," went on Irwin. "That commitment will restrict his educational and job opportunities — his entire future on this earth. A decision for Christ is a supreme commitment."

"Frequently, the believers asked what we had to sacrifice to be a Christian in the United States. In spite of the restrictions and persecutions, we came away feeling that the believers were the only truly happy people in Russia."

"We went on this trip to encourage the believers, and we came away encouraged and challenged in our faith. We had an opportunity to share with 10,000 Russian believers."

The next morning was to be our last in Russia. The tour had come to an end. I got up with Jim for an early-morning stroll in Red Square. The first rays of sunlight were just breaking over the surrounding brick and stone buildings, casting their warmth on the cooled cobblestones. I enjoyed it with every breath, taking it all in with my eyes. This was the very heart of the Soviet Union. I beheld the magnificent architecture, the Kremlin complex, St. Vasily's Church, the Museum of Natural History. Sunrise on Red Square is beautiful.

Deep down, I sensed my return to Moscow would be a long time coming. I looked down at the cobblestones and every stone seemed to cry out in unbelief, doubt, cynicism, mistrust and godlessness. The system was cemented in disbelief. Every man distrusted his neighbor. Every tourist was a potential enemy. Every believer was a harmful ingredient to society. The church was a reactionary force, slowing down the march of Soviet society towards its utopia.

At the Sheremetyeva International Airport, we were ushered out of the bus and into the terminal building.

I was approached by a customs officer who asked, "Are you Mr. Haukka?"

"Yes," I said, surprised.

"Where are your bags?"

"Here."

"Take them aside," he ordered. "Have your group step this way. You stay here for the moment."

"Here we go again," I sighed. I knew this would be my farewell.

After a superficial inspection, the rest of the group moved on to passport control and to the waiting Finnair aircraft. When they had all been cleared, my bags were lifted onto the inspection counter and opened.

The uniformed customs agents conducting the inspection were asked to step aside. Four KGB agents in civilian clothing took over. I thanked God that I had the sense to surrender all my films and tape cassettes to Jim enroute to the airport. My suitcases were thoroughly checked a couple of times.

"Do you have anything on you?" asked the commanding officer.

My answer was negative. Experience told me that any attempt to conceal anything from customs in situations like this were totally futile.

"Follow me!" he instructed. I was led to an enclosed area away from public scrutiny by a plainclothed KGB agent. It was a makeshift booth, assembled for temporary use. The walls were made of a kind of prefabricated material. A curtain was drawn over the doorway in place of a door. Unauthorized persons were not allowed into the area. I did not see anyone else the whole time I was in the area.

"Take everything off," I was instructed by the man. Each article of clothing was pressed through fingertips, square inch by square inch as I stood there in my birthday suit feeling this whole episode was ridiculous.

"I see you don't believe me," I said, my usual line at Soviet customs.

"We just want to make sure your words coincide with the truth," he said back at me through clenched lips.

The body search was thorough. One agent ran his fingers through my hair, while another stuck his index finger between each toe, separately. This would have ejected any piece of paper that may have been placed there.

The plane was now late, but these men were not in a hurry. After the search, I repacked my one suitcase and camera case. I was not yet free to proceed to passport control or get on the plane.

A line of six men out of uniform formed a half circle around me. A rare honor.

After a lengthy rebuke, one of them made the announcement that I had been dreading for a long time.

"You have visited our country a total of twenty-seven times," he said. "You have gravely misbehaved on this trip. I hereby inform you that your travels to our country have come to an end!"

"Hereafter, every entry point to this country will be closed to you. It will be futile for you to attempt to enter."

The words, "Your travels have come to an end," hurt me. I understood that the iron gates of the country of my calling had finally slammed shut.

"What have I done to deserve this?" I asked, feigning ignorance. I was well aware of what was going on. There was no legal offense to my name. The reason was ideological and religious. But, the authorities could never admit to such a reason.

"You know full well what you have done," said the officer.

I protested once more with the little emotional strength that I had left.

"Think about it carefully," he snickered. "Then, you'll get it!"

"Well, if I have done something offensive, it was unintentional, and I ask you to forgive me, if such be the case. The State has offended me on my travels many times and I am ready to forgive you," I said turning the tables on the man.

Forgiveness. The word did not compute in the minds of these KGB men. I could see from their facial expressions that they were fervently searching their "memory" in quest of a definition for the word. Finally, someone spoke up.

Breaking the silence, the officer said unemotionally, "You have offended us one time too many. Just go and do not ever try to return."

Obeying my orders, I grabbed my bags and moved toward passport control. My KGB escort handed my passport and visa to the soldier at passport control. The solider was not up to speed. The irritated KGB agent ordered the soldier out of his cubicle. Seizing the stamps he processed the documents angrily.

By the time I entered the aircraft, everyone was already in place, seatbelts fastened. I dropped into my seat mentally and physically drained. I was beat, but happy. Twelve unforgettable days in the USSR were behind me. Even though I was now banned, I felt pleased that I had been terminated during such a trip. It had been a visit of a lifetime for me, during which thousands upon thousands had been touched with the Gospel of Jesus Christ. I was honored to have been a part of it!

Jim had witnessed to over 10,000 in the actual church services. Tens of thousands of others would learn his story by audio cassette and pictures bearing his autographed, "With God's love from the moon, Jim Irwin."

Russia needed to hear it. Objective science and the Bible are not contradictory, but compatible. Faith in God was for space age people, too.

Jim Irwin saw me as I took my seat and leaned across to me and said, "You made it! For a moment, we thought we would be leaving without you."

I smiled. I also had thought they would be leaving in the McDonnell Douglas DC9 without me.

Chapter Twenty-Three

The Shackles
Come Off

I quickly settled back into my life in Helsinki with Laura. As the ministry continued to grow, pressures in program production caused us to continually pray for more staff to assist us.

But we faced a serious problem. During the Brezhnev era in the Soviet Union, Russian-speaking staff were hard to come by in the West. What made it even more difficult for us was that we needed Russian children for our drama programs, children that were to be found only in Russia.

"Lord," I fervently prayed one day as Laura and I kneeled side-by-side in our studio before the start of our workday, "please send those much-needed Russian speakers our way according to Your will. We know that the harvest is truly plentiful, but without the proper manpower, we cannot do the job well."

The answer came most unexpectedly. I was in a deep sleep when the phone rang early one Saturday morning. In a blur, I reached through the darkness, switched on the bedside lamp and picked up the receiver.

"Hello," I murmured hoarsely, as Laura turned her back trying to avoid the intrusion.

"Mr. Haukka," said a female operator from the Finnish telegram office. "You have a telegram from Archangel, Russia. Should I read it to you?"

"Um, yes, please do," I said desperately trying to clear my blurred mind.

"It says, 'The answer is positive", It was signed 'Inkeri'," she said.

I thanked the woman and hung up.

"What was that all about?" asked Laura, as she turned around in bed.

"It was a telegram from your sister, Inkeri," I told Laura. then I blinked twice and looked at Laura. Pow! Then it hit me like a bowling ball.

"Laura," I said with excitement rising in voice, "they have received permission to come to the West. The family must have got their exit permit." By now I was almost shouting with excitement.

Laura had fully opened her eyes by now and was instantly awake.

"What telegram?" she questioned as she eased herself out of the bed and reached for her robe. "What more did it say?"

I could provide no further answers.

"Thank you, Jesus," was all I could exclaim. "Praise God, they are free to leave."

We both fell silent, staring at each other in stunned disbelief.

"What do we do now?" Laura finally asked.

We realized that seven people would soon be arriving from Russia, including Laura's mother, Eva, her sister, Inkeri, Pavel, her husband, and their four children. We were renting a two-bedroom townhouse. Where on earth could we put them?

The Voronenko family was looked upon as troublesome dissidents by the Soviet Communist government. They had gone through some tough times because of their deep faith in God and their refusal to compromise their beliefs. The spiritual darkness in which they lived in northern Russia was beyond description. In such a terrible climate, the inhabitants there consumed record amounts of alcohol. The crime rate was high and morality was low. Churches were few and far between.

Archangel, situated on the shores of the Arctic Ocean, was home to a population of half a million souls. There was one Orthodox church in the city and it drew a consistent number of worshippers despite the government's active discouragement of religion. There was no evangelical church in the area.

Pavel was an unregistered minister and had decided to defy the authorities by holding worship services in his home in Archangel. The house was not much more than an oversized shack, but Pavel was determined that it would well serve as a church. His decision immediately drew the fire of the local KGB. From the very outset, they sent the militia to break up the services. Pavel was arrested on several occasions in 1978 and was fined heavily for his lawbreaking.

The cumulative sum of these fines exceeded Pavel's monthly wage. So, instead of picking up his paycheck as a welder, plumber and general handyman on the local construction sites, he would pick up a note stating that he owed money to the city for unpaid fines. Having to continually pay the fines would have meant death by starvation for Pavel's family of six, but church members "stood in the gap" and pitched in to cover the family's living expenses.

The authorities did not restrict their punitive measures to fines alone, however. Once, in the month of October, the threshold of the severe winter in the north, the local police showed up at the Voronkenko home, cut the power line to the house and sealed the wood-heated stove. This effectively left the family without heating and lighting in their home.

When Pavel came home from work, he found the family shivering in a cold house. Without hesitation, he went outside and reconnected the power line and removed the seals the police had placed on the stove. As a result of his action, the fines escalated.

One day, a delegation of five municipal officials showed up at the front door of Pavel's house. As Inkeri opened the door, she was confronted by a doctor, a policeman, a school teacher, a city council member and a school board member.

Her heart missed a beat when she saw the scowls on their faces. Inkeri was aware that there had been a dispute over her request that the children not be made members of the Young Pioneers, the Communist youth organization. Inkeri had said that she did not want them to wear the uniform of the organization, which included a red bandana around their necks.

The group roughly pushed past her and began checking everything in the house. They searched the children's toys, their clothing and the sanitary conditions in the house. As Inkeri observed their frantic activity, she was relieved that they had found nothing they could latch onto. The group was confused and could not agree on the next course of action.

"We are leaving," said the uniformed police officer, "but we will be back in a couple of days."

As the door slammed behind them, Inkeri, and Eva, her mother, sprang into action. There was no time to lose. The children had to be sent into hiding immediately.

The children were happily playing out in the yard when Inkeri called them to come inside. The children's few necessities and clothes were packed into a bag and a sixteen-year-old girl believer from the congregation was hastily summoned to take the children to a destination that would be unknown to the authorities.

Inkeri's farewell kisses and hugs would be the last contact she would have with her offspring for months to come.

Having worked out their differences, the delegation returned a few days later. With them they had a confiscation permit. By that time, the little fugitives were a thousand miles from home and running for their lives.

When the group discovered that the children had gone, the policeman wrote out a protocol of what happened and gave Inkeri a copy. The delegation again disagreed among themselves about what action to take, so they issued a written warning that the next time the children were present at a religious service, they would be removed from their parents.

Inkeri then sent a telegram to Vera, her and Laura's cousin, asking her to come to Archangel. After being briefed on the situation, Vera sent a plea for support to Christians in the

West. She initially sent her request to the Slavic Mission in Stockholm and they took the news and distributed it to all European mission organizations working in the Soviet Union as well as to the major Swedish daily newspapers.

Soon, the story was published in a number of national newspapers outside the USSR. In addition, Inkeri and Pavel sent a petition to Party Chief, Leonid Breznev in Moscow, asking him to intervene in the situation.

When I heard of the difficulties the family were experiencing in Archangel, I called Pavel from Sweden, and he gave us the highlights of the story. Later, tourists from the West were able to provide us with the full story.

The furor in the West had caused considerable discomfort to the authorities in Archangel. A department of the KBG fired off a query as to what the uproar was all about.

Another knock came on the front door of the family home. Inkeri went to the door and was confronted by an angry official from the local city council.

"What is all the noise you are making in the West?" he demanded to know with his voice quivering with animosity.

He was met with blank stares by both Pavel and Inkeri, so he tried the soft approach.

"You know that we never intended to take away your children," he said. "They may return home. We will not harm them."

But the couple were not falling for that ploy. "Of course you want to seize the children," Inkeri countered boldly. "I have a document to prove your real intentions."

"What document?" he spluttered. "Give it to me."

"No," said Inkeri, spotting the trick. "It is my only proof of what your intentions were. You cannot have it!"

The man again promised that the children could safely return home and withdrew his demand to see the document. With that, and with the perception that this document was the family's proof of the authorities' true intentions in case they reneged on their pledge not to harm the children, she sent word to the secret place of refuge that the children were now free to return home.

* * * * *

Laura and I continued to sit on the bed in our home staring at each other in open-mouthed wonder. The telegram had taken us by total surprise. We spent the day in a state of happy shock, and that evening over a cup of tea, an idea was birthed and took flight against any measure of earthly logic that we might have.

God had planted an idea in Laura's heart. When she had first suggested it I thought that she was kidding. Has Laura forgotten the political system in her country? I thought to myself. There was no physical way the family and Eva were going anywhere.

But, Laura was serious and insistent. We agreed in prayer that an invitation would be sent, via official channels, for them to come to Finland.

The exodus of the family from northern Russia would have to be a miracle of major proportions. But that supernatural event was to take place. After months of apparently insurmountable obstacles put in their way by the Soviet authorities, the day came when they received their exit visas from the local KGB, and they boarded the train taking them to the West—and freedom.

* * * * *

The Helsinki-bound Soviet Railways train crossed the border on October 4, 1984, carrying the first Russian family to be given "landed immigrant status" by the Finnish government since the end of World War II. The party included Pavel, Inkeri, their four children, Afanasy, Aida, Andrei and Anna, and Eva, Laura's mother. (Her father had previously died in Russia.)

Details started to fall into place once the family arrived. Temporary shelter was provided by IBRA Finland. They moved into a flat that was to be sold, but was available for a few months. We decided to build a duplex for both families.

The local bank extended a warm welcome to them by providing a special low-interest loan for the building project that

I personally guaranteed as the family obviously did not have a financial track record in the community. A parcel of land was awarded us through a municipal lot lottery. This was a practice used for distributing almost unavailable zoned land to large numbers of resident applicants. The lottery was a draw. Only a few lots were available, but anyone in the area could submit his or her name for the draw. If their name came out of the box, they were then given a first option to buy the best lot in the draw.

After our names came out of the box, the duplex was to be constructed by a missionary builder who gave freely of his time and energy to complete the project. It was a wonderfully exciting time for all of us. At last, Laura was reunited with her kith and kin.

Meanwhile, the trickle of letters to the ministry, although heavily censored by the Soviet authorities, began to build up. There was just enough mail to afford us a glimpse of the power of international radio. The ministry was bearing precious fruit.

The first salvation report to reach us through the "Iron Curtain" was from Slavomir. In a moving letter he wrote, "Jesus has saved my soul. Thank you for telling me about how He died for me. I love Him and I want to tell others about my Lord."

Then, another young man, Andrei, 17 years of age, wrote from Leningrad, "I thank God that I belong to Him. He saved my soul not long ago. [Before that] I lived an immoral life. I was a sinner. But through your programs, God has showed me that He loves me and wanted to save me and that He died for me. The Holy Spirit ministered to my heart. I have given my life to Him and have been forgiven all my sins. I am so happy now."

THE WAY TO FREEDOM

The teenager added, "I am telling you this so that you would know how powerful God is. I now know that there is no other purpose in life outside of Christ. I am ashamed of my sins and when I now pray, tears of repentance and thanksgiving flow. You helped me to see the truth. You showed me the way to freedom. I found God. I am so happy because Jesus now lives within me!"

Soon letters began to pour in from cities all across the USSR. I would pray each time the letter carrier would come to our box and place the mail into our box, that just one would eventually come from Laura's home city, Petrozavodsk.

One day, I picked up a small stack of letters. A quick perusal of them revealed that there was just one that day from the Soviet Union. My heart leapt as I saw it was from Petrozavodsk. Hurrying on inside, I ripped open the envelope in Laura's presence.

It was from a woman called Irma.

"Read it to me," uttered Laura anxiously. "It will improve your Russian."

I started in. "Arthur, my son," Irma wrote, "brought me to your radio program. It was a great event in our lives. He said he found your broadcasts while he was scanning the dial. Never in all my life will I forget that night.

"From that night on, we have a new life that cannot be compared to the old. My son brought me to the Lord through your broadcasts. You gave us the most precious gift — the knowledge of Jesus who is now our Savior!"

Perhaps the most remarkable news came from southern Russia. The envelope contained photos and a letter that told us of a whole village of eighteen people who had committed their lives to the Lord by listening to our radio broadcasts. These new converts requested Christian literature which we were happy to supply. God was giving us the necessary encouragement we needed to keep us at our happy task of sharing the Good News with the people of the Soviet Union.

They, too, had found the way to freedom!

A Super Miracle

Chapter Twenty-Four

A Super Miracle

As Laura and I sat in the office of CBN Executive Dr. David Clark in Virginia Beach, Virginia, at the beautiful facilities of Pat Robertson's Christian Broadcasting Network, we had to pinch ourselves as we learned more about a new animated Bible video series.

"I see. So you would like to dub the series into Russian," said Clark, a delightful man, expressing a keen interest in what was happening in the USSR.

A friend of mine in Helsinki had seen the series on video cassette and had told me, "Hannu, you need to see this. It could be used in Russia. I know that you and Laura have a deep concern for Soviet children."

Although Laura was producing a drama program for radio aimed at children, we knew it wasn't enough. The warfare being waged for the souls of Russian children demanded heavier artillery from our side. So, on a trip to the United States, we decided to drop into the CBN Regency-style headquarters from which the popular "700 Club" was televised live daily.

As we concluded the agreement to dub the series into Russian, I was fully aware of the obstacles we faced in putting this product into the hands of children in the USSR.

Russia was a mysterious land still fanatically hostile to any form of child evangelism. Children in Soviet society were considered to be "most holy," a precious segment of society not to be tampered with or contaminated by dissident ideology. Teaching children about God was absolutely forbidden. It was a punishable offense. Because Sunday schools in the country were only operated clandestinely, we would need to smuggle the tapes in.

We were aware that the Communist leaders of the Soviet Union had done a sterling job in bringing education to the country. When the Bolsheviks came to power in 1917, no more than thirty percent of the population could read. One of the first decrees signed by the Soviet leader Lenin established universal, coeducational, free education.

Implementing such a decree was especially difficult, however. Among the problems the government had to face were the huge size of the country, with its eleven time zones, and the existence of at least 100 languages (some even without an alphabet) spoken by the people of what were becoming the new republics of the Soviet Union. Again, in some sections, such as the Central Asian areas, schools had never existed. Therefore, there was no broad base of educational equipment or buildings.

Before the Revolution, education was generally only available to a privileged few. In 1913 only six percent of the total population of czarist Russia were in schools of any type. As late as 1920, only forty-four percent of the population at the age groups of nine to forty-nine were literate. By now the literacy rate had grown to more than ninety-nine percent.

In the face of such difficulties, the progress that was made before the 1980s was remarkable. Soviet preschools at that time had an enrollment of about fourteen million — more than twice the number served by day-care centers in the United States.

Ten years of education are compulsory where available (five years of elementary and three of lower and two of higher secondary.) Statistics at that time suggest that 97% of the youth will obtain some secondary education.

The underlying philosophy of the Soviet educational system was then to produce citizens loyal to the party and capable of contributing to the material growth of the State.

That is why all children were required to join the Young Pioneers, a movement that espoused the Communist philosophy. The children were expected to wear, as part of their school uniform, the red bandana of the Young Pioneers.

Typically, Soviet education was designed to meet the needs of the State. Pupils were taught the principles of Marxism-Leninism along with their academic courses. The Gorbachev reforms reemphasized this.

As I sat there with David Clark, Gordon Donaldson, the vice-president of IRR/TV, and my wife Laura, I remembered how God, whenever He planned to perform a mighty work, chose to use things that were insignificant and meaningless in the eyes of man.

When God spoke to Elijah, He was not in the hurricane-force wind, the earthquake or the fire, but rather in a gentle whisper. A palm-sized cloud had brought a mighty rain strong enough to stop a horse and chariot. Abraham was promised a multitude of descendants through his only son Isaac. David slew Goliath with a stone and a sling. Five thousand people were fed with five loaves and two fishes.

As we left the CBN office, I smiled to myself, and Laura saw the slight smile cross my face.

"What is so funny?" she asked.

"Well, don't you realize that we have no equipment for the job and there's no money to buy it?" I responded.

We had taken a step of faith and we did not expect the Finnish board to back us in helping to raise the funds. We were convinced that we had to get this product into the hands of Russian children.

A TOTALLY IMPOSSIBLE SCENARIO

The location of our ministry was in Finland, and few in North America had even heard of our work, but I sensed we would ultimately need the backing of North American Christians.

I knew that God had spoken to my heart about television to the Soviet Union and we had to start somewhere. So, when I returned to Finland, I paid a visit to a bank near the studio.

"Yes, can I help you?" asked the manager of the branch office.

"I hope so," I began tentatively. "I need a $100,000 loan."

He looked at me like I was an alien that had been featured in an American tabloid. Then he asked me what I wanted the money for, so I explained about the "Superbook" project and said I needed it to purchase some video equipment, a VTR, a monitor and an audio mixer.

"If I can get these items, I can launch a spectacular video series on the Bible called Superbook," I told him, as I held my breath for his response.

The banker was amused. He wrote a few notes. Momentarily he spoke up. "Interesting. I think I can manage the loan. What do you have in the form of equity?" he asked.

I was stumped. Obviously, this was an issue that I had not considered.

"I am sorry, sir, but I don't have any," I told him honestly. "All I can offer is my signature." I knew that was not really worth much to him.

Without a flicker of emotion, he then told me, "Mr. Haukka, our bank knows you as a man of a reliable ministry." About a week later I was in his office again to sign the necessary papers.

"What kind of a payback schedule can we work out for you?" he asked pointedly.

BLIND FAITH

I hesitated for a moment, and then in blind faith I replied, "Four months!" I did not have a clue as to where the money

191

would come from. Then a verse in the eleventh chapter of Hebrews came to mind. It was, "Faith is being sure of what we hope for, and certain of what we do not see." I was absolutely sure of what I hoped for and I was unshakably certain of what we did not "yet see." God would provide. I knew that more than anything, God loved the children of Russia.

With the loan secured, I went out and ordered the few pieces of required equipment. The dubbing process began. After a short time of hectic round-the-clock editing the first episodes of the animated Bible were completed, and I began to arrange for them to be taken to underground church groups in Soviet Estonia and the Leningrad area. What happened next was a sovereign move of the almighty God. We were about to witness the greatest miracle the Soviet Union had ever seen in the spread of the Gospel in that country.

It had been another long day at the studio and I was ready to go home. As I began to look forward to my evening meal with Laura, the phone rang in the control room.

It was one of our friends who had just returned from Leningrad.

"Hannu," he said excitedly down the line, "Have you heard that a portion of 'Superbook' has just been shown on Leningrad TV. It must have been seen by millions of viewers."

"What?" I exclaimed. "There must be some misunderstanding." I asked him to repeat what he had just said. He did, and I could not believe my ears. Then I stood there numb with the receiver in my hand and staring out the window. A portion of the Bible had been transmitted on Communist-controlled State television.

At that time, a camera crew from Leningrad TV was on assignment filming a documentary on religion in the USSR. They visited the home of a Christian family in that city and, when they arrived, they noted that the children were enthralled as they watched a video program. It was one of the first episodes of Superbook.

"That's not a Soviet production," remarked the producer as he eyed it with keen interest. "Could I borrow it?" he asked.

Divinely a two-minute excerpt was included in the documentary when it was aired on Leningrad TV. The Leningrad channel was the third largest in the USSR, right after Channels One and Two. Its programming was seen throughout Russia proper and many of the other republics with an estimated viewership of seventy million.

The viewing audience reacted immediately and spontaneously. Telephone calls and letters poured into the offices of Leningrad TV asking what the excerpt was and whether more of the kind could be shown.

I felt my heart would explode with sheer joy. I thanked my friend and replaced the receiver in its cradle. I ran over to Laura's office and blurted out the news, hugging her as I related the story. For a long moment we just stood there, looking at each other in disbelief. Tears started to spill down onto her cheeks as she listened to my explanation of what had taken place.

"God has just engineered a miracle of massive proportions," I shouted and also burst into tears of joy. That was April 26, 1989, a date that will forever be emblazoned on my heart.

But, that was just a foretaste of what was to come.

Only a few months later Leningrad TV signed a contract with us for the Superbook series (in Russian) to be aired as a weekly program. The first time in the history of the Soviet Union that a Christian television series was broadcast. The various episodes had been on the air for about eight weeks when again, very late one night, the phone rang. This time it was was a liaison officer for Channel One of Soviet Central Television in Moscow.

"Central TV has just seen the 'Superbook' program on the Leningrad channel," the man told me. "They would like to negotiate a contract with you to show the series on the nation's largest TV channel."

I had done my research and was aware that this would seen by an audience of over two hundred million viewers.

"Call me back with your terms," he said as the line went dead. I didn't know what to make of it.

"Unreal," I exclaimed to Laura who was in the kitchen preparing a late evening meal. "You will never guess what is up now." I took a deep breath and held it. "National TV wants the series," I blurted out in disbelief.

We had followed the events in the country for years as we, along with other Christian broadcasters had toiled with little tangible results, broadcasting the Gospel to the Soviet Union by radio from outside the country.

Christian television was totally out of the question. It had never been done. The Communist party was still in power. Now the news about our video series on television inside the country was overwhelming.

That day finally arrived when the greatest miracle in Soviet Television history happened at the end of May 1990 when Soviet Central Television started telecasting the Bible in animation to the nation. However, not all went smoothly. Four weeks into the series, senior Communist party officials woke up to what was happening. Something odd was going on in their country and they did not agree with it one bit. They were coming home after a hard day's working "fighting for world domination" only to have their grandchildren approaching them with the words, "Grandpa, guess what? Do you know how the world was made? God created it! I saw it on TV."

With blood boiling, these party officials fired off fierce protests to the chairman of Soviet television demanding that the programs be yanked off the air. After seventy-two years of Communistic, atheistic indoctrination, this could not be tolerated. They would not have their grandchildren teach them Who created the world.

The chairman responded by ordering the program to be discontinued. But what God has destined, man cannot change. Members of the children's programming department stood up to their boss and threatened to resign from the Party and discontinue their work if they were forced to take Superbook off the air. Faced with that ultimatum, the chairman backed off and the series continued to air.

The program soon became the most watched in the USSR. By the time the last episode was set to air, we had developed a yearning to discover how much the Russian children had absorbed of what they had been watching. So we put together three simple questions and aired them after the last episode. No one was prepared for the scenario that was about to follow.

194

A MOUNTAIN OF MAIL

The phone rang at our IRR/TV counseling center in the center of Moscow.

"Hello," said a man with an agitated voice. "This is the central post office. Would you please come over quickly. We need to talk to you."

A couple of our staff arrived to see the confusion in the post office. It was an incredible sight. A mountain of mail spread all over the floor of the building. They were deluged with letters.

"You asked us for a post office box," started the supervisor. "You don't need a post office box. You need a post office! Now take all of this mail to your office, sort it and return the letters that don't belong to you."

The mail flow broke all records in Soviet postal history. Thirty thousand letters came in on the first day after the program and within four weeks, over a million had arrived.

Parents and children alike wrote in. The central theme in every letter seemed to be, "Tell me more about God." For the next six months our staff along with hundreds of volunteers, responded to each of the over one million letters, sending each child and their family, The *Story of Jesus*, a booklet specially prepared for Russian kids. God was truly a God of miracles. If He was to take Jailbird Joseph and make him prime minister of Egypt, then He had done just the same thing again by taking a special video cassette and putting in on national television to a whole Communist nation.

No previous program on Soviet television had ever triggered such a response from its viewers.

There was more to come. CBN caught the vision.

As I dangled 24"x 36" color pictures blown up for the occasion in front of the cameras on the 700 Club, Pat Robertson seemed awestruck. For a moment he was speechless, realizing the magnitude of what was happening.

"Wow, ladies and gentlemen, we have got do something for Russia! Look at this! Something is happening over there and God wants us to be a part of it!

Soon I was in Russia with CBN vice-president Michael Little (now president of CBN) in a taxi racing down Koroleva Street in Moscow towards the Soviet Television Center. I had come to know Michael as man with a heart for the world, burdened with the vision of reaching the nations, using television as a tool.

We would soon be sitting in the grand studio of that vast television center for all of the USSR. *Superbook Party* a joint-project with CBN was being videotaped in front of an audience of 500 kids and adults. It would ultimately trigger millions of letters in response.

Laura had the privilege of delivering the message and giving an altar call on air to the whole nation that day. She preached on the prodigal son. Russia's millions needed to come back to the Father in heaven after 72 years of godless living.

The impact of this simple cartoon series was truly awesome. An American television crew visiting an elementary school in Leningrad wanted to know how Christianity was faring after decades of atheism.

"Do any of you know who Jesus is?" he asked the children. He was greeted with a unanimous "Da" (Yes) from all of them.

The teacher who had watched this was surprised at their response.

"How do you know about Jesus?" she spluttered. "This is illegal."

The reporter then asked her to try and discover where the children got their knowledge. "From *Superbook*," all shouted.

When the teacher then asked what they all knew about Jesus. One little boy stood to his feet and said, "We've learned how Jesus came, who He was, why He died, and why we have eternal life."

The TV anchor was overwhelmed at the impact that Superbook had made on the lives of these Soviet children.

Not long after, one of the Soviet diplomats that I had spoken with at the embassy suddenly arrived at my office. "Hannu," he smiled, "what are you going to do now?"

"Excuse me?" I countered, not really understanding what he was referring to.

"Well, remember you told me at the embassy that your goal was to reach every person in our country with your message [about Christ]," he started in. "Now you've achieved your goal. *Superbook* is a phenomenal success. Everyone in the USSR knows about it. You've achieved your life's goal. You can retire. There's nothing more to do."

I laughed. But should I really consider retiring?

The miracle unfolds—a million letters received in one month from TV viewers in Russia.

Hannu presents CBN founder, Pat Robertson with a token of their joint ministry of reaching out to millions of Russian children.

The signing of the first ministry program contract with Russian State TV.

The contract is signed! Over 200 million people would see 52 choice Bible stories on nationwide TV.

Chapter-Twenty Five

A KGB Agent
Defects

Night had already fallen when Vladimir Grigoriev and his wife, Lyudmila, stepped off the bus into the parking lot of a local Bible college near Helsinki.

Vladimir was the son of a Soviet naval officer. He was lightly built with dark, curly hair and a dark mustache. He appeared on that first meeting to be an intelligent guy as he greeted me from behind some distinctively Soviet-made eyeglasses. Dressed in blue jeans it was hard to tell that he was Russian if you first saw him from behind.

"Hello," said the 30 year old man warmly, extending his hand to Laura and me. His curious, dark eyes twinkled with excitement as my grip was accepted by him.

We had come to know of this interesting couple through correspondence. Vladimir had written to us that he had "stumbled across" our programs while checking across the dial of his shortwave radio. What he heard had caught his attention, he stated, and this had aroused his interest in God. Consequently, Vladimir had written to us and we had developed a two-year file of his fascinating letters.

This Russian had told us that he had attended a service in Tallinn and had there made his decision for Christ.

"I would very much like to come and visit you with my wife," he had penned in one letter.

Laura and I had decided that a neutral party should send him and Lyudmila the necessary invitation. This would increase his chances of getting an exit visa from the Soviets. Laura and I were both considered to be hostile towards the ideology of the USSR. The Soviets classified all western radio ministry "ideologically dangerous."

After spending a short time with our Finnish friends, the couple joined us at our studios and for the next ten days we enjoyed their company as they helped us with our work.

Vladimir, because of his extraordinary command of the English language, proved especially useful translating scripts from English into Russian for me. Lyudmila, on the other hand, was a good typist and so she busied herself typing scripts for us. It was a wonderful blessing for us as qualified Russian staff were hard to come by in Finland.

Lyudmila and Vladimir spent their days in the production facility and their evenings at the nearby Bible school. The school had graciously given the pair free room and board.

As the projected departure day for Vladimir and Lyudmila approached, Lydia, our senior staff member who was responsible for travel arrangements, pressed me for a definitive departure date. The couple had not told us exactly when they intended to return to their home across the border.

"Don't worry," I told Lydia. "They will inform us when they are ready to leave."

I had other things to attend to and so I did not give the matter another thought. Out of frustration, Lydia then turned her attentions to my wife.

"Laura, can you please help?" she asked urgently. "We've got to know when they will leaving, don't we?"

Laura was, by now, also becoming concerned. In between recording sessions, she stopped me and said, "Hannu, please find out when they are leaving." Reservations needed to be made and we had to know the dates.

Feeling the pressure, I set aside my work and stepped into the room where Vladimir was busy translating.

"I am sorry to bother you, Vladimir," I started, "but could you please tell me your departure date? I need to confirm your tickets."

Just as I spoke, I saw a puzzled look sweep across his face. Vladimir stood up and lightly grabbing my arm, motioned me towards the main entrance.

"Let's go outside," he suggested.

I still suspected nothing. It was not unusual for a Russian believer to insist on having a talk outside on the street. In their home country, they were afraid to talk about sensitive issues inside a building because of the fear of bugging. As far as I was concerned, Vladimir was just insisting on the same procedure, even though he was abroad. The instinct for caution seemed to be in the blood of all Russians.

By now we were in the street and Vladimir turned and looked me straight in the eyes.

"We are not going back to Russia," he said with little emotion in his voice. "We have decided to go on to Stockholm."

I stared at my guest in disbelief. *This must be a joke,* I thought. I blinked not realizing exactly what he had just told me.

"What is passport control like between Finland and Sweden," he asked as my mouth was now agape. His question had jolted me out of my bewilderment. He was serious! "You have no idea of what you are doing," I blurted out. "Vladimir, do you have any idea as to what kind of predicament you will be putting us in with the Soviet authorities?"

I paused, "What's more, if you are planning to defect, you had better understand that you are choosing a difficult and lonely path.

"You don't speak Swedish and you don't know anyone in that country," I tried to point out. "Western Christians cannot be compared to Russian believers in hospitality and friendship.

"Besides, you can't do this to us. We arranged for your visit. You have been at our production facility for ten days and everyone knows you have been here, including both Soviet and Finnish state security. Now you are talking of defecting to Sweden."

The Russian stared blankly at me as I continued, saying that we had established good relations with the Ministry of Religion and our relationship with the Soviet authorities had been steadily improving. This was important to us.

Even as I spoke, I could tell from Vladimir's faraway expression, that he was not listening.

"Hannu, I cannot explain my decision," he finally blurted out. "All I can do is to repeat that Lyudmila and I are not returning to the Soviet Union."

Admitting defeat, I went inside and quietly told Laura the shocking tidings. "We should reserve them tickets to Sweden, not Russia," I uttered in disbelief.

The news had not yet sunk in with her. "What do you mean, Sweden?" Laura shrieked, agitation written all over her face.

"It's a mess," I declared. "I'll tell you later."

With that, we packed the Grigorievs into my car and drove them the short way to the Bible college dormitory where they had been staying.

The college is located on a peninsula on Lake Vanajavesi, a beautiful, restful setting that also served as a recreational area, used by joggers in the summer and skiers in the winter.

The four of us got out of the vehicle and walked around the protruding land area. We paused at the sauna.

Laura decided it was her turn to try to dissuade the defectors from their plan. But her attempts bore no more fruit than mine had.

"We cannot go back to Russia," insisted Vladimir. "We cannot explain why yet."

He then asked, "When do the ferries leave?"

Both Laura and I decided that attempting to talk them out of defecting was a waste of time.

"Hannu, could you accompany us to Stockholm?" Vladimir asked. "I fear we will not make it without a guide."

"No way," I responded. "What do you take me for? We broadcast Christian programming to Russia. They know all about us." It is in the interest of this ministry to have good relations with your government."

I tried to explain that, as their visas were expiring the next day, the Soviet Embassy in Helsinki would immediately be in contact with our authorities to ask about their whereabouts. "Right after that, the Finnish Security Police will contact us," I said. "And what will I tell them? That we put you on a boat to Sweden? Great! Just great...! No! I am definitely not taking you to the boat."

Shaking with anger, I added, "If you want to defect, then do it without my help."

Vladimir looked sad. "Couldn't you at least take us to the harbor?" he asked somberly.

Feeling a stab of remorse for being so harsh, I decided to apologize for my outburst. But I knew that I could not relent.

"No," I said resolutely after expressing my sorrow for my anger, "I'm sorry, but I can't even do that!"

At that moment, Aki Miettinen, our IBRA Finland national director, walked into the yard where we were now standing. Aki had been a captain in the special forces responsible for security along the 1,000-mile long Finnish-Soviet frontier.

I knew it was only a matter of time before Finnish Security came knocking on our door so I decided it was better for him to be appraised of the whole story, and quickly filled him in.

"What?" shot back Aki. "To Sweden?"

Both Aki and I had heard and read a lot about people escaping from Russia. Aki had been specially trained to handle illegal border crossings and defectors. Now we had two living specimens on our hands. Aki, like myself, knew we had to be careful for the sake of our ministry that was located in a politically sensitive area of the world.

After some searching, Aki found a car that was traveling in the direction of Turku, one of the three Finnish port cities connecting the two Scandinavian countries with each other. Aki explained to the driver where his passengers wanted to go. Then Vladimir and Lyudmila got in and began their life-changing journey. The getaway had begun. The couple were determined to never again return to "Mother Russia."

Speaking through the car door before leaving, Vladimir had just one more thing to say. "If you want to know why we are not returning to the Soviet Union, have a friend come to the Stockholm Harbor and I will them him what I could not tell you here."

I nodded in agreement. With that the car pulled out of the driveway and headed west for the highway to Turku.

I was ready for bed the next evening, when the phone rang. It was Alvar Prosen, the publishing director and literature coordinator for the Swedish Slavic Mission. On this occasion, the usually talkative Alvar was unusually terse.

Without greeting me, Alvar began: "Hannu, tell me what you know about your friend, Mr. Grigoriev?"

I had never heard Alvar's voice so serious.

"Well, not much," I responded. "I know he was a listener of ours. We've been in correspondence with him for a couple of years. He said he had become a Christian and he's been working in our studio for the past ten days. He speaks good English, too. I guess that's about it."

Alvar was silent. "Take Laura, and catch the next boat over to Stockholm," he suggested urgently. "We have to talk!"

With that, Alvar hung up. I stood there for a long moment looking at the receiver and then replaced it into its cradle.

* * * * *

As our car pulled out of the hull of the ferry onto Swedish soil, I looked for Alvar. There he was, standing by the bus stop. I pulled up beside him, killed the engine and got out of the car. Alvar's complexion was a whiter shade of pale and he was shaking like a leaf.

"Vladimir Grigoriev is a KGB agent," he began, as Laura joined us. "He has served the KGB for twelve years and now you have allowed him into your studio for ten days."

As he uttered these words, I felt my legs turn to rubber. I stared at Alvar. Then events of the previous ten days began to race through my mind. I was frantically recollecting Vladimir's every move. He had had access to the computers as well as our archives, he had read the correspondence. "What could he have seen?" I asked myself.

"Let's go," said Alvar, as his voice snapped me back into reality. "Vladimir wants to talk to you. There's something he needs to tell you directly."

"Where is he now?" I asked, trying to gather my whirling thoughts.

Alvar directed me to his office where he said I could speak with Vladimir in privacy. He dialed a number and soon Vladimir Grigoriev, the KGB agent, came on the line.

"Hannu," he told me, "I have worked for the KGB in their department responsible for religion. I was with the infamous 'fifth section' which keeps tabs on all ideological activity hostile to the state. To us, Christianity was definitely hostile!"

Then came the shocker.

"I was sent to Finland to gather intelligence on your ministry, with which it could be destroyed. Hannu, of all foreign missionary groups involved in the USSR, the KGB fear only two: you and Earl Poysti, but you are the number-one enemy!"

He paused and then added, "You are doing a great work. Please continue and do as much as you can. You cannot understand how much your work means to the people of our country."

I was dumbfounded. I tried to breathe normally. How could this be possible? This was 1989, the period of Mikhail Gorbachev's *glasnost* (openness) and *perestroika* (restructuring). And here was a man who was telling of KGB plans to destroy a Christian ministry.

A SPY COMES IN FROM THE COLD

Vladimir's voice came back on the line. "Hannu," he said, "please forgive me for what I have done to you. I have spied on you for many years. I lied to you when I said I had been a Christian for five years. I have been a Christian for only a year. I became a Christian while working on your case. I can no longer continue to work for the KGB and so I cannot return to the Soviet Union. If I did return, they would either shoot me or put me into a mental asylum."

We were both aware that Soviet psychiatric institutions were houses of horror. Completely sane "patients" were forcefully "treated" with drugs and brainwashing until they completely lost their minds. A sentence to a mental asylum was much worse than capital punishment.

I discovered from him that in 1978, Vladimir had obtained damning evidence against workers at a clandestine Christian printing facility. The workers were arrested and condemned to several prison terms. One of them, a Jew, had received a five-year sentence, while another was dispatched to a psychiatric institute.

Vladimir's hands were stained with the blood of his own countrymen. Recruiting westerners for the KGB was among his duties as well. He also divulged details of his surveillance of our ministry inside the USSR. He knew everything about Laura's trips to the Soviet Union and had a dossier on her movements inside the country. He also knew of her meetings with believers while in the country.

Vladimir also seemed to know the names of a number of so-called "moles" operating in Soviet churches. A "mole" is an undercover KGB spy sent into the Christian community or a church, disguised as a believer, for the task of gathering ideological intelligence. This "mole" would report on all foreign guests in a church service. He would also attempt to gather information on the private lives of influential individuals. He also admitted to having served as a "mole."

We continued talking and I told him that I was interested in the duties assigned to him regarding his trip to Finland, the trip from which he would never return.

Vladimir told me that he was to supply his superiors with precise floor plans of our studio, the location of our computers, the names of Soviet believers we were linked with. He also had been instructed to gather information about our financial base. In addition, Vladimir was given the duty of planting miniature wireless microphones in various parts of our facility.

In a whisper, I told Vladimir, "I forgive you for Jesus' sake. I just pray that you will serve Christ with the same fervor and dedication as you have served your former employer. May God direct your paths according to His will."

I hung up. I was able to thank God for at least one thing. Our ministry had not been in vain. If I was "enemy number-one," then that meant that our broadcasts had found fertile ground, open ears and open hearts all across that great land.

Chapter Twenty-Six

Never Through Away A Business Card

Adversity in our ministry not only came from the KGB. We also faced problems from the inside as well. The upper levels of administration in our ministry were not exercising sensitivity in what I felt God wanted us to do for Russia. Finances, I was told, would not be forthcoming for the broadcasting of the Gospel to Russia.

One example of our difficulties was evident in the surprising exodus of the Voronenko family from Russia.

Funds were needed for their relocation in Finland. They were to become an integral part of the ministry.

In a frantic effort to raise some funds for the family's immediate needs, I decided to contact all of our friends and acquaintances. I went to my office drawer and dug out every business card I could find as well as other names I had put in my address book. Then, on that day late in 1984 and with much prayer, I began to compose my first-ever appeal letter

209

and then mailed it to all on the list, a total of about forty names. Gordon Donaldson, a former civil engineer and city planner in Calgary, was one of the few that wrote back. He responded by pledging to give $15,000 for the purchase of a minivan for the transportation of the family. I was surprised by his generosity as he did not know us well, and I did not know him at all.

I discovered later that years earlier — sometime between 1959 and 1960—Gordon Donaldson had received a vision from the Lord. Its emphasis seemed to be directed by the Spirit of God towards the USSR. "I can recall some great times of prayer when everyone else in the family was asleep," he said.

"The Cold War was still at its full fury and, under the circumstances, any widespread Gospel work there seemed totally impossible and ridiculous to contemplate.

"I can remember one night facing east towards the Soviet Union and praying that God would raise up an individual to be used in a mighty way by the Lord. Immediately, I was caused to swing around and face the west and I received a strong impression that the individual I was praying for was then approximately six years old. A strong love for Finland was from then on developed in my heart."

Gordon and his wife Marie, began to seek out Finns living in Calgary and met up with John and Liisa Römpötti, who happened to live close by. There, the two of them, learned more about Finnish culture and history, particularly its uncertain relationship with the Soviet Union.

THE VISION

At the end of the Western Canada Chapter of the Full Gospel Businessmen's International fellowship meeting in Calgary, FGBI founder and president, Demos Shakarian, was invited to speak at the local Full Gospel church, which was attended by Gordon and Marie.

"Following a powerful message Demos invited all those who wished for prayer to come to the front," recalled Gordon. "I joined the group in front of the platform. When Demos prayed for us, I received a vision. In it, I saw a map that seemed to have tongues of fire emanating out of southern Finland and directed to the Soviet Union; to the south and southeast. When the vision was finished, Demos came to me and asked about my experience. I shared it with him and the whole congregation, and because of his Armenian descent, he asked if the fire had extended as far as Armenia (in the southern USSR). I replied that I couldn't be that specific, but that it seemed to cover most of the Soviet Union."

In 1966, Gordon Donaldson attended the Full Gospel Businessmen's International convention in Stockholm, Sweden, and in conjunction with the convention, a group then traveled on a Soviet boat from Helsinki to Tallinn. He said, "We visited three churches in Tallinn in three days and found things there very tight."

After working for the city for thirteen years, Gordon said he received an impression from the Lord that he should quit his job, and make an impromptu trip to Finland.

"I cashed in my pension funds and arranged the trip," he said. "That fall, I flew to Finland and took a bus from Helsinki to Orimattila to visit John and Liisa Römpötti. They were in their homeland for a lengthy stay due to the illness of Liisa's father.

I had the idea that I could import some Finnish products into Canada, so I asked John to accompany me to seek out possible items. We traveled to many factories and before I left Finland, I had registered an import company which I called Finnish Imports."

However, when he arrived back in Calgary, Gordon Donaldson partnered with a Jewish investor who helped to establish a land development consulting business, so he dropped all thoughts of importing goods from Finland.

I had received Gordon's card sometime in 1981 after speaking at a service at a world missions convention sponsored by the Finnish Pentecostals in Calgary. It was surprising that Gordon was there at all, since he spoke no Finnish. He had come after hearing about a national revival in Finland and was interested in hearing more about it.

"John Römpötti had invited me to the conference, but I had declined after he had told me that everything would be conducted in Finnish," explained Gordon. "He was somewhat persistent, so I agreed to come to luncheon where a Finnish evangelist spoke."

I was there on a trip with Laura to garner support for IBRA Finland and, at the service, Gordon had apparently been touched by what he had heard via the English interpretation.

Curiously, four years later I still had his business card, even though I could not recall what Gordon looked like. Months after the Toyota van was purchased, Pavel and I visited Calgary as part of another support-gathering tour of North America, and Gordon had assisted us by setting up a few meetings in his home city. As we met with some of our Finnish friends in Canada in Gordon's home in January of 1985, he recommended that we register a charitable organization in both Canada and the United States. That was destined to be a God-blessed suggestion of immense value in days to come. He also suggested we call the ministry, International Russia Radio/TV.

Gordon, who already had established a missionary foundation in both countries, agreed to handle IRR/TV Canada under the umbrella of his foundation. "God was beginning to get my attention again for Finland and the Soviet Union," he explained.

Gordon instructed that his California non-profit corporation changed its name to International Russia Radio/TV.

"As I didn't have any experience in setting up a U.S. organization to handle a potentially large mailing list, I discussed the matter with Ray Barnett [the founder and president of Friends in the West] in Vancouver. He said I should meet Dan Wooding [co-author of this book] with whom he had just written, Uganda Holocaust, a publication about the terrible years of the church in Uganda under Idi Amin."

"I went to Los Angeles and sought out Dan Wooding", said Gordon. "He referred me to Thomas Ed Steele, who was very interested in helping us, but the start-up costs were too much for us to contemplate. A later meeting was arranged with Steele at the National Religious Broadcasters convention in Washington, D.C. I was in on that meeting and I was able to convey to him my burden for souls in the USSR. Nothing came out of that meeting, so we continued to struggle to establish a constituency to fund the ministry."

Back in Finland, the outreach had dramatically outgrown the facility. The office we worked out of was extremely small. But this building had served the ministry well. One setback, however, was its geographical location—we were in the middle of nowhere.

Every room in the house we were using, was occupied. The shower room had even been transformed into an audio duplication center. Even the sauna served as a warehouse for blank cassettes.

TIME TO MOVE

I began to sense that it was time to move. Our staff, too, had grown from the days when only Laura and I were involved. God had called a wide assortment of people to work alongside us. One of them was Lydia, who had quit her job as a translator for the Finnish Air Force. She had joined our staff and we felt honored to have someone of such a constructive spirit with us on the team. Then there was Mauri Itkonen, a commercial salmon fisherman from the west coast of British Columbia. He had sold his 40-foot troller and signed up with us as an audio technician. His cool-headedness, his seemingly pleasant personality, fitted in well into the high-pressure atmosphere at the studio.

Those whom God calls He also tests. My kid brother was a fitting example of this. John's call to the ministry was different than many others. He had flown over from Canada to Finland for a visit in 1982 to see Laura and me. I had promised to take him up north to Lapland on a salmon fishing trip. I had told him about the quality of the fish in that unique area of the country.

"I have even heard of salmon weighing up to fifty pounds," I told him as his eyes became big as saucers.

"I would like to see that," was his skeptical response. As our boat zigzagged across the powerful Teno River in the rushing waters high above the Arctic Circle, the land of the midnight sun, in quest of a trophy fish, I shared with John an experience I had had in West Germany, a month earlier.

It was the early eighties, two years after the radio ministry to Russia was launched and God was casually planting the seeds of a television ministry to that great land in my heart. It would take years, however, for those seeds to germinate.

I had been asked to serve as a replacement for one of our denomination leaders at a Christian television conference in West Germany sponsored by the Crossroads Family of Ministries, I told John, as the ice-cold river crashed by us. Leaders came from all over Europe and I was there to represent Finland.

I can distinctly remember standing in a session alongside those dignified middle-aged European leaders, wondering what I was doing at a television conference. I was only involved in a radio ministry, so my attendance did not make any sense to me.

I continued by telling my brother that Christian television to Russia was virtually impossible.

I told John, "My being there had to be a mistake." I went on to explain that I felt an inner voice quietly speak to my spirit. It was God and He told me, "Hannu, at this time, you do not understand why I have brought you here. But in days to come, you will understand why."

I said to John that I had tried to absorb all that was being said. I dutifully made copious notes for the Finnish brethren. But I left the conference, not understanding the significance of my attendance, I said. "I only knew that God wanted to introduce me to television. Perhaps some day, I pondered, I would understand. Maybe I would be part of His plan for our ministry."

John had his amateur video camera with him and, as he listened to me, was busy shooting the gorgeous pine tree scenery as we fished our way along the river.

I usually did not make a practice to petition God for fish, but our rather costly license was running out and we had not had a bite for three days. Just as I was in fervent, silent prayer, the rod by John's leg violently bent over.

"It's a big one," I exclaimed triumphantly. John hastily lay down his camera and began spooling in the monster to set the hook. We frantically changed positions in the narrow canoe-type boat as I took the rod. John manoeuvred the boat in the tricky current and then at the right moment when I had played the fish to exhaustion, John took the gaff hook and accurately struck the silver slab in the head and pulled it into the bottom of the boat. It weighed in at forty-three pounds.

He then picked up his camera and videotaped the flapping salmon, with myself spread-eagled over it to stop it from jumping back into the river. John also took a still picture with his camera of me holding up the four-foot long fish. I later framed the photograph and attached the words, If God hears prayers like this, then surely He will hear us when we ask Him for the souls of men.

This great catch gave me an idea. "You know, John, I think we need to start collecting good interviews on videotape for Russia," I told my brother. To do so, we set up a whirlwind tour of the U.S. and Canada. Having rented a worn out television camera, we booked ourselves on twenty-two flights in twenty-one days, which put us zigzagging across the continent. Our budget dictated that we use red-eye specials and we often slept on our camera equipment in various airport terminals.

We did however, come up with some great interviews with prominent Americans like Pat Robertson of the 700-Club, Jim Irwin of Apollo 15, Jack Lousma of the 5th space shuttle mission and other NASA scientists who were professing Christians, as well as David Wilkerson, author of The Cross of Switchblade.

The enemy was not happy with what was about to unfold. In the spiritual realm, hell must have sensed that God was planning on a miracle of unheard of proportions for the Soviet Union just down the road. And the enemy wanted to stop us before the plan got off the ground. One of the most hair-raising experiences was our flight from Norfolk, Virginia, to Buffalo, New York. Our flight almost never arrived.

Flying at an elevation of 33,000 feet, the aircraft had just begun its descent into the Buffalo area, when the plane suddenly encountered wind sheer, causing the aircraft to plummet uncontrollably. I had the sensation that my insides were rising in my throat. Mothers and little children broke out in hysterical screams. Immediately I knew what was happening, and I began to count the seconds, One thousand, one...one thousand, two... The aircraft continued to drop for eleven seconds. Suddenly, the aircraft found air under its wings and, with a violent shudder, it stabilized and attempted to ascend. No sooner than it recovered, the plane hit another pocket of wind sheer and it dropped again. I glanced over at my brother John, who was sitting beside me. His eyes were closed and his knuckles were white. Later he told me that he was saying his last prayers. Then it happened again and by the time we had pulled out of our third violent drop, I glanced out of the window. I could clearly see the tree tops just below us. We were no more than a thousand feet above ground. Chaos was rampant in the aircraft. Strangely, there was no explanation on the intercom until we landed. But as we walked out of the jetway into the terminal area, we saw the captain and co-pilot comforting hysterically weeping mothers and children saying, "It's all right...we're okay, it's over now."

The enemy was determined to cut short this dynamic ministry to Russia, still in its embryonic stage, but God had other plans. Four years later, John was ready to pack his bags and moved his family to join us in the ministry in Finland, to spearhead what I thought would be a booming demand for our videos for the Soviet Union. This view was possibly a little presumptuous. I was not the architect of the ministry, but God was, and He controlled events in the USSR and the timetables. When John finally arrived in the fall of 1986, he was surprised to discover that we still had no finances for equipment and there was no office space for him. The small facility we worked out of was small and overcrowded already.

We borrowed a desk from another worker, and John found a phone that had not been in use for a decade.

PAINT IT BLACK

The environment was not uplifting for him. Instead of editing videos, John was spending more time mowing the lawn and weeding the studio garden, than doing what he planned to do: help make TV and video programs. During this period of frustration, John wrote, "All of a sudden, it seemed like I had made a mistake by moving to this bitterly cold country from my comfortable life in western Canada. Not only was it cold, but the food was very expensive and the people were not very friendly towards us 'aliens.' Also, the cost of living just about broke me every month that passed by. And those long, dark nights, were so depressing! I came to work when it was dark and went home when it was still dark. And if I failed to look out of the window at just the right moment, I would miss daylight altogether."

John stated that he had come to Finland thinking God was leading him into this video ministry. "It's been six months and I do not see a single piece of video equipment around," he added. "Now they are short of funds and cannot pay my salary on schedule. How am I going to explain this to my family? Have I been deceived in my own thoughts? Maybe it was not God's plan for me to come."

As part of his responsibilities, John wrote hundreds of letters to friends and ministries in the West to try to garner funds for the ministry. It was the day of small beginnings. John's call was being tested, as was my vision. But God would not allow us to be tried beyond our limits. Slowly funds started to trickle in. So did the very first pieces of video equipment. These were the beginning labor pains of the birth of television ministry to the Soviet Union.

Soon John's desk was cluttered with video equipment. And, eventually, his salary was paid on time. Our immediate concern now became more space. We needed a bigger facility.

I sensed in my heart that big changes were on the horizon. I approached the Finnish board and presented the need for a new, expanded facility, that could better serve our present ministry. I told them that we need a place where we could have a television studio and editing facility. To the board, this sounded ludicrous. There was no sign of an opening in the Soviet Union for a television outreach.

The reaction was negative. Some of the board members thought I was hallucinating and had finally gone completely crazy. "I think we need to transfer the whole operation to Helsinki," I told the board members. "It is the only logical location for an international ministry to the USSR."

Sadly, my presentation, only split the board even more. The members divided into two camps and, for two long years, they slugged it out. The in-fighting made me decide that I needed to regroup. But I was watching the older men of God fighting for power within their denomination. The new facility, they knew, would cost at least a million dollars. I estimated that the TV equipment alone would cost $500,000.

It would be unfair to say that the board unanimously opposed my vision. Some were cautiously supportive of a larger facility and the move to the country's capital. The following twelve months were, for me, a time of anguish and inner suffering. The board members would not even commission us to look for a lot on which we could build a facility. I could see the flow of natural growth engineered by the Holy Spirit was being damned up, with pressure mounting on all sides.

On October 30, 1987, I wrote in my diary, *We found a lot...this is the rainbow after the rain after a dark night. We will have a crucial board meeting next week. Lord, we can do nothing alone. Almighty God, You can! Let them understand Your will for this ministry!*

Sadly, the board meeting was for me a total disaster. And then in December 1987, an annual meeting was called to discuss the issue of our geographical location. I wrote in my diary, *Today we had a board meeting. Today the board* [of IBRA Finland] *torpedoed the loan for additional equipment, the plans for* [our] *TV ministry, and put in question everything else. But Lord,* [these] *steps backwards will not depress me. My trust is* [only] *in You. My faith is in You. The ministry will either stand or fall in You. If it is true that You love my generation, the ministry will prosper."* I also wrote, *"Brother Kai* (the chairman of the board) *has a spirit of strong faith, a spirit of Godly faith."*

God had the last word. He broke the deadlock. Resistance within the board slowly crumbled and on March 15, 1988, the group again convened. This time it was moved and agreed that the ministry be transferred to an area that was best suited for unhindered growth of the ministry. By May, the board had come around to unanimously support the horizons of the ministry to Russia. But, at that time, none of us had any idea what that would mean.

Co-founder of IRR/TV, Gordon Donaldson with his wife Marie. God's provision of encouragement and inspiration in trying times.

Hannu's brother, John, dubbing the first "Super Book" video with IRR/TV's first piece of video editing equipment in 1987.

Chapter Twenty-Seven

Embassy Encounter

No one in Privolnoye in the Stavropol territory of the Soviet Union could have guessed on that fateful day of March 2, 1931, when Mikhail Sergeevich Gorbachev was born, that he would one day change world history.

Well, possibly no one except his proud mother, a committed Christian who had pledged to pray each day for her son. She continued with that practice for more half a century and had watched as, at the age of 54, he became the youngest man to head the government of the Soviet Union since Joseph Stalin came to power in the 1920s. Gorbachev was also the first general secretary of the Communist party not to have served in the armed forces during World War II.

Many years later, Mrs. Gorbachev glowed with joy on the day she saw on Soviet State television that in 1985 her Mikhail had succeeded Konstantin Chernenko, the Soviet leader since 1984.

Those of us watching from the West, were initially suspicious when Gorbachev began initiating a series of policies ultimately aimed at a complete restructuring of Soviet society. The terms *glasnost* (openness) and p*erestroika* (restructuring) came into common usage as the man with a birthmark on his head tried to undo seven decades of economic stagnation and political repression. Through a restructuring of the constitution and open elections, Mikhail Gorbachev also brought a measure of democracy to Soviet politics.

One of his policies must have pleased his mother greatly. For in the late 1980s, Mikhail Gorbachev pledged to increase religious freedom for all believers in the USSR. For seventy years, the Soviet Union had attempted to eradicate all concept of God from Soviet society. But, in 1988, Soviet leaders realized they had failed, so they put the process into reverse.

Gorbachev, a self-confessed atheist, was being used by God to pave the way for the beginnings of unheard of freedoms for the peoples of the Soviet Union. And in 1988, Gorbachev supported The Millennium Celebrations of Christianity coming to Russia.

"The choice of Moscow as the focal point of the celebrations, before the guests departed to attend subsidiary events in other cities, was itself controversial," recalled Michael Bourdeaux, the founder of Keston College in England, a highly respected center for the study of religion and communism in the Eastern Bloc countries.

Writing in his excellent book, *The Gospel's Triumph Over Communism*, Bordeaux went on to say, "After all, the city-state of Kiev had been the eye of medieval civilization long before the foundation of Moscow and it was here that Prince Vladimir had descended the steep slope of the River Dnieper, ordering his courtiers and subjects to be baptized after him and to embrace the new faith. The river bore away the jettisoned idols and the images of paganism."

Bordeaux said that the choice of Moscow for the whole week of the celebrations (June 5-12) reminded Ukrainian believers that it was the Russian Orthodox Church that played the dominant role in the land. "It had even justified and benefited from the liquidation of the Ukrainian Catholic Church in Western Ukraine over forty years earlier."

Churches across the USSR, Protestant and Orthodox alike, were busy organizing "high visibility" celebrations. Many international speakers were invited including Billy Graham.

I also received a couple of invitations, and hopes of a return to Russia after ten years of exile were revived.

Over the years, I had made couple of futile attempts to visit the Soviet Union. One attempt was a visa-free cruise to Tallinn from Helsinki. Visas were not required, but name lists had to be submitted to harbor authorities seven days prior to the arrival of the cruise ship. This gave the Soviets ample time to go over the names and spot unwelcome tourists. Raimo, my best friend, had succeeded in going ashore this way on a previous occasion, so I decided to give it a shot.

When the boat arrived and the passengers started to disembark, my name was called over the ship's PA system.

"Would Mr. Haukka report to the Captain's office," came the words I had been dreading to hear over the loudspeakers.

As I walked into the office, I was met by a high-ranking officer of the Soviet Frontier Forces.

"Hannu," he said as he smiled disingeniously.

I was taken aback. Why was he using my first name?

"Hannu," he pressed on, "I am sorry to tell you that you cannot disembark. You will have to remain on board."

Even as he spoke, I had figured out that he had used my first name as a way of letting me know that he knew exactly who I was and what I was up to.

I had watched sadly as the others left the ship, exchanging their passports for a special landing pass at the inspection desk.

It seemed that every checkpoint was closed to me just as the KGB had promised ten years earlier. No official reason for my exile was ever issued by the Soviets. I personally knew of dozens of others like me who were in the same situation and none had ever received an official statement concerning their "persona non grata" status. Everyone on the list that I knew had been caught smuggling Bibles.

WINDS OF CHANGE

But, as Mikhail Gorbachev's new Russia was emerging and bringing the consequent winds of change to the USSR, I decided to try again. A Soviet diplomat at the Helsinki embassy, told me that he could investigate the reasons for my expulsions. He indicated that a change in my status might be possible.

"Why don't you apply for a change in status?" he suggested helpfully. "In order to do so, you will need a statement from the Finnish Police saying that you have no criminal record."

He grinned as he added, "You don't look like a felon to me."

I smiled back and was pleased to hear this. However, I did not believe it would be that simple to get my status altered. The embassy official said that he did not know why I had been blacklisted.

On my next trip to Helsinki, I decided to drop off the police declaration that I had secured. Aki, the new director for the Finnish radio ministry had accompanied me.

As I stepped out of the vehicle outside the Soviet Embassy, I told Aki that I would be "back in five minutes." I added, "I'll just leave the document with the receptionist and then I will be right back."

Inside the consular section, however, a male secretary glanced at my paper and, unexpectedly asked me to "wait a moment."

A minute later, two diplomats wearing matching expensive black pin-striped suits, white shirts and jazzy ties, appeared.

They wanted to talk to me, so we they motioned me into another room, away from the consular traffic.

The government officials were not only smartly dressed but also exceptionally well-mannered. After exchanging formalities, one of them got straight to the point.

"Mr. Haukka," he began, "you have been forbidden to enter the Soviet Union for some time. What, in your opinion, is the reason for this?" I paused for a moment and then responded, "Well, I visited the USSR in June of 1978 with an American astronaut called Jim Irwin. We went to several churches. The astronaut talked to the people about faith in God. There were a lot of young university students present. Your authorities were not yet ready for that kind of a visit at that time. I was held to blame for the trip and was exiled."

The diplomats listened intently and did not attempt to correct my interpretation of the events I had recounted.

"Are you a Christian?" the other diplomat finally asked.

"Yes," I responded, puzzled. I would have thought they would have already known that, as the embassy not only had a dossier on our ministry, but also had been involved in the Grigoriev spy scandal.

"Do you really believe that God exists?" he then asked, giving me a wonderful opportunity to share my faith with them. This man had probably never heard of anyone talking about a personal faith in God.

"Absolutely," I affirmed brightly. "As a matter of fact, I not only believe God exists, but I also believe in the Bible. It is the foundation for my life."

"Tell us how you found this faith in God?" The man then asked. The question came out a little hesitantly as if there was a doubt about what I had said.

I related to my hosts about the turning point in my life when, as a young man in Canada, I needed to make a decision as to what I wanted to do with my life.

"I asked myself the question whether or not I wanted to live without God or for God?" I stated. "I understood that without a relationship with God, I was spiritually lost. And because of my sins, I was condemned to unending separation from Him. I knew I needed forgiveness and realized that Jesus, God's Son, came to tell people that God forgives sin and died on a cross to atone for our sins. When I realized that fact, I asked God to come into my life and to forgive me for the wrong I had done in my life."

The diplomats nodded their heads with great enthusiasm. They then abruptly changed the subject.

"We know that you regularly broadcast religious radio programs into our country," said one of the men. "What is the ultimate goal of this activity?" The question was posed politely, but I knew that the wrong reply could cause me further problems.

We were still dealing with a communist superpower called the Soviet Union. During the old Cold War days, this would definitely have been a hostile question. So I tried to interpret the true purpose of their question.

But then I felt the Holy Spirit whisper to me, "Do not fear to respond directly and tell them the way it is—openly and frankly." A strange peace came over me as I spoke up. To their surprise, I responded with a counter question.

"How many people are there living in the Soviet Union?" I asked them after taking a deep breath.

Not expecting my response, the diplomats thought for a moment and then one of them responded, "Two-hundred-and-ninety million."

I smiled. "The ultimate goal of our ministry is to tell two hundred and ninety million people in the Soviet Union, WHO Jesus is, WHY He came down to this earth, WHY He died on a cross, WHY He shed His blood. He did it so that two-hundred-and-ninety million Soviets would know that they have forgiveness of sins through the blood of Christ and that through Jesus Christ they can have peace with God."

The men were by now captivated, and listened intently to my every word.

"I believe that everyone has the right to hear the whole story of salvation. Once they have the facts, each must then make his or her own decision to either believe or not believe. It is everyone's freedom to chose. Everyone makes his own personal decision."

The men stared at me without speaking. I could see bewilderment written all over their faces. After a long silence, one of them spoke up.

"But, we have the Orthodox Church in our country," he nervously pointed out. I could see that he was obviously grappling for words. It was obvious that no one had ever told them what they had just heard. God's love for mankind seemed to be headline news to them.

At one point, one of them, said, "Hannu, we cannot believe the way you do. We have been given an atheistic upbringing. Our education prohibits us."

I could see that they were struggling against the conviction of the Holy Spirit. A spiritual battle was being waged for their souls.

When our conversation got a little close to home, Anatoly, one of my interviewers in astonishment noted, "Do you think that in such a short time you can persuade us to be Christians? Somehow those words seemed to be peculiarly familiar. They were from the Book of Acts. The words of King Agrippa to the Apostle Paul. I beamed with joy.

The conversation lasted for about ninety minutes. A tap on the shoulder of one of the men ended our conversation.

"I knew it," he said as a third diplomat approached him to call him back to his consular duties. "It seems that just when something really interesting happens, you always get called away," he said as he rose to his feet. Turning to me, Anatoly looked at me with a warm glow in his eyes. "Hannu, we are talking about the same thing. We are both advancing peace, aren't we?"

"Yes," I said as I stood up. "Peace, indeed. But there must be peace first here on the inside," I added, pointing to my heart. "Only then can there be peace around us."

"You will make it a long way in life," said Anatoly smiling. With one last look, he shook my hand and reluctantly walked out.

I glanced at my watch. I had been gone for an hour and a half and Aki was still waiting for me outside in the car. Nikolai and I concluded our conversation and I promised to send him some Christian materials.

Returning to the car, I radiated with joy. I had never before enjoyed the chance to witness to two so apparently receptive Soviet government officials.

"I thought they had already shot you," said Aki as I stepped into the car.

"I've just returned from the Acts of the Apostles." I grinned. "I'll tell you all about it on the way home."

A few weeks later a phone call from the Soviet Embassy in Helsinki brought news that I had been longing to hear for many years.

"Hannu, your name has been removed from the lists," a contact there told me. "You are free to travel."

I didn't need a second call. In February of 1989, the "Iron Curtain" of the land of my calling, began to swing wide open. Laura and I decided to first go to Leningrad and Petrozavodsk.

In a happy daze, I looked out of the window of the Soviet coach and I could see the familiar frontier zone. Nothing had changed in eleven years, but somehow I felt I was coming home. The same unpainted wooden houses, on a slight tilt to one side. The expressionless Viborg railway station and sad to say, the same tired, almost lifeless looks on the faces of milling crowds.

Still, I was aware that something had changed. My own presence on Soviet soil was evidence of that turnaround. As I watched the customs officials climb on board they, as usual, seemed from another planet. With glasnost in the air, I did something I had never done before. I openly noted in my customs declaration that I had a personal Bible with me. I did not want to be accused of smuggling.

After all, it was my first trip after eleven years of exile. The customs official looked at the form and smiled at me. "Mr. Haukka, you don't have to declare your Bible," he said softly. "The times have changed. You are now allowed to bring Bibles into our country."

I smiled in bewilderment. His words were like music to my ears. "Times had certainly changed," I echoed to Laura as he found the fifty evangelistic video cassettes in our luggage.

"There is no problem," he said. "Please take them in with you."

As I stepped off the train in Leningrad, I stopped to look at the masses of people milling around the platform. I looked deep into their faces. Tears came into my eyes. These were the people that I had been ministering to by radio for the past decade. Some of them had undoubtedly heard our programs, and through them, I prayed, the voice of God.

Chapter Twenty-Eight

The Victorious Cross

"You are making up for lost time," said the bemused Soviet diplomat at the Helsinki embassy, as I picked up my third visa in almost as many months to visit his country.

God had given us a new facility and brought us to the Finnish capital for an increasingly effective ministry to Russia. As we made the move into the new facility in January 1990 in the heart of the city, I knew that our work to the Soviet Union was now really beginning. For television in the Soviet Union was opening up to the Christian message.

Actually, it was fast becoming the former Soviet Union with Mikhail Gorbachev hanging onto power by a thread. Without realizing it, his policies had actually been the precursor to the end of communism in his massive land, as well as the satellite states of Eastern Europe. He had even ended the decade-long war by pulling Soviet troops out of Afghanistan.

Mother Russia was definitely on a new course. But where would it take her?

By February of 1991, all fifty-two episodes of Superbook had been shown on Leningrad TV. Earlier in the fall, I had visited the Baltic states of Estonia and Latvia. The State TV in both republics had signed contracts to air Superbook. The speed at which this was taking place was taking my breath away.

We were already beginning to take this former super-power by faith!

But the extraordinary chain of events did not end there. With the help of the supporters of International Russian Radio\TV in North America, God had provided the funds for us to "tool up" with state-of-the-art equipment like cameras, an edit suite and a beautiful studio. The total investment was close to $2.5 million.

"I think we are ready to move forward," I beamed as Laura and I gazed in awe at what had been installed in our Helsinki facilities.

OPEN DOORS

The doors just kept opening up for us. In May of 1990, Leningrad TV began airing our direct ministry program. Just as for Superbook, large amounts of mail poured in from all across the former USSR, from people hungry for more knowledge of the God they had been told by their government did not exist. Now, the very same media was allowing us to tell the story of Jesus for the first time since Lenin seized power back in 1917. We had good reason for jubilation.

We continued to sign contracts with other major channels such as Ukrainian State TV, with an audience of 40 million. This was followed by Belorus (White Russia), Karelia, as well as Moldova, Armenia and Georgia TV.

The vision to reach the whole of the USSR was coming to pass. I had to pinch myself as all of this took place. It was too good to be true. "How long will it last?" was the question I kept asking myself, as did my colleagues in the ministry.

The answer came on the morning of August 19, 1991. I arrived at our headquarters in Kerava to be greeted by the chairman of our Finnish board, Kai Antturi.

Kai was visibly shaken. "Have you heard the news?" Kai asked me.

"What news?" I had not seen the morning papers yet.

THE COUP

"There has been a coup in Moscow," Kai said, his voice quivering with emotion. "Gorbachev is under arrest. A revolutionary council has assumed command of the country."

He explained that the Soviet media had announced that Gorbachev was "ill" and that Boris Yeltsin was holed up in the Russian White House, the parliament building, two miles from the Kremlin.

This information hit me just as if someone had thrown a pail of water in my face.

"What do think?" asked my friend. "Do you think this will mean the end of the ministry?"

I could not think. I was in total shock. The television ministry had just started and now it looked as if the hard men of the Kremlin would deal a death blow to it.

I said that I felt that we needed to pray for the situation. We all held hands in a circle, and I began to implore God to intervene. "Oh, God," I cried out, "please don't allow this coup to succeed. I pray that you will halt it and allow Mikhail to come back and continue in the path of freedom. There is still much to be done."

As tears were now pouring down my reddened cheeks, I heard a familiar inner voice that I had come to recognize as the Holy Spirit: "Hannu, this is not the end. Do not be afraid. The crisis will pass. Time will be extended for the ministry."

I opened my eyes and loosened my grasp on the hands of my colleagues. Wiping the tears from my eyes, I said firmly, "Brothers, this is not the end. This is just a warning shot."

WORDS OF FAITH

I was saying things that, given the circumstances, had no validity. But I felt that God wanted me to verbalize the faith that He had given me at that moment.

Still, message or no message from the Lord, I was devastated with this turn of events. I needed to sit down and pray.

As I sat in a chair, I wondered if God would allow something like this to happen without giving us his forewarning.

"Let's get the staff together," I told Laura, who had by now joined us in the studio. We prayed again.

Even as we implored God to stop the coup, the news streaming out of Moscow was all bad. All programming on Soviet radio and television had ceased with the exception of communiques from the revolutionary council and the screening on television of old black and white films from the 1930s.

When the news of the coup d' tat broke, a recently converted employee for Soviet Central TV was with us in Helsinki, helping us with program production. As she learned the news she broke down and began to weep openly.

"This is terrible," she sobbed. "If they succeed, we will return to an era that will be just like the Stalin times."

We did no work that day, but remained glued to Finnish television. As the details poured in, the negative implications to our outreach were becoming ever more apparent. These were hours and days of emotional torture for all of us.

On Tuesday, the second day of the coup, and a full day before the Western media received wind of the imminent failure of the power grab by the hard-liners, we were told of a turn of events.

At 4:55 p.m. Moscow time, I was speaking by phone to Yuri Burov, the senior director of Soviet Central TV in the Russian capital.

"Hannu," he said brightly, "things are looking better. "I can see tanks below my window. The building is surrounded, but we are feeding the soldier boys and letting them use our toilet facilities. It will be over soon."

He said that informed sources had told him that seventy percent of the Russian people were on the side of Boris Yeltsin, who was then Gorbachev's right-hand man, who was taking a valiant stand to try and stop the takeover by the Communist leaders.

"More and more soldiers are defecting to his side," he went on," he continued. "Don't worry about the situation."

Even as he spoke, Boris Yeltsin had stood on a "friendly" tank outside of the Russian White House, and denounced the

231

plotters to the cheers of those that were manning the barricades. Citizens had streamed to the White House and thrown up makeshift barricades as tanks took up positions.

As I put down the receiver, I uttered out loud my innermost feelings, "Thank you, Lord, for this encouraging message."

Minutes later, the line was open to Virginia Beach, Virginia, where I was speaking with Pat Robertson, the founder of the Christian Broadcasting Network, and two officials from the U.S. government who were speaking to Pat from Washington, D.C., by satellite. I told them the news I had just received from Moscow.

"The crisis will soon be over," I said firmly.

To my dismay, one of the American political analysts spoke up. "I don't agree with what was just said," he stated, "the information we have just heard is not accurate."

That night, hours later, came the assault on the Russian White House by the Soviet troops. I continued to pray fervently, tormented by the thought that God had not really spoken to me.

By morning, however, it had become clear that God had intervened in the affairs of the Russian people. Something had gone dreadfully wrong at the revolutionary council headquarters as the vodka had flowed freely and they had toasted their short-lived victory for Marxist-Leninism.

Their plot had failed and Mikhail Gorbachev and his wife Raisa had returned from his exile in the Crimea.

The Soviet Union would continue on its path of reforms— but for how long?

Hours after the victory, people stormed the Lubianka, the infamous headquarters of the KGB in downtown Moscow and toppled the huge statue of Felix Dzerzhinsky, the founder of the dreaded KGB from its plinth and replaced it with a simple wooden cross.

Underneath, a Russian Christian had hung the inscription which said, "The cross is victorious."

The ample bosom of Mother Russia had finally emerged from more than seventy years of xenophobia and the broken empire was on a new course as it sought to break free of its past like a butterfly out of its cocoon. The superpower known as the Union of Soviet Socialist Republics would never be the same. It would soon cease to exist. In its place would rise a fiercely nationalistic Russia and the Commonwealth of Independent States (CIS).

IRR/TV Studios and International Headquarters, 150 miles from the Russian boarder.

Chapter Twenty-Nine

A "White House" in Russia

The imposing figure of Boris Morgunov, a Soviet Jew, stood beside camera two in our main studio in Helsinki and began to "count me down" on his fingers. He indicated, five, four, three, two, one, and then whispered into his head set, "VTR roll," and pointed to me.

"Good evening," I said, looking straight into the lens of camera two, which was operated by Boris Lazarev, a former senior Soviet Central Television camera operator who had traveled with Leonid Brezhnev and Mikhail Gorbachev, "shooting" their public appearances. Boris had since miraculously come to Christ through our programs and then joined our staff after leaving his prestigious position.

"Welcome to tonight's show which we have dedicated to those of you who have written to us with your questions about faith in God, the Bible and the role of the church in Russian society," I continued.

I was seated on a couch, with a large oval table before me. On it, piled high were stacks of letters representing millions that we had received from across the former Soviet Union. All of them contained pointed questions such as, "How can I believe in God?" "Who is God?" and "If He really is alive, how should I pray to Him?"

Sitting directly across from me was Laura, my lovely wife and co-host who had, for the past seventeen years, tirelessly corrected my every pronunciation error in the Russian language. That period had meant "blood, sweat and some tears" for me, but tonight she smiled as she knew that the fruits of her efforts had paid off as she listened to my nearly flawless Russian delivery.

"Laura, you have some extremely interesting letters before you, so please introduce us to the people who have written in and tell us what their questions are," I said.

My wife picked up some of the letters and then turned to our guest ministers, Alexei Bychkov, a leading Baptist from Moscow Central Baptist Church and Leonid Odessky, a prominent Pentecostal, also from the Moscow area. Both were Board members with the Russian Bible Society.

"Here's a question for Alexei Bychkov," Laura said, as she gently turned her attention towards the veteran Christian leader. "A viewer from Novosibirsk asks, 'What is salvation and how does one experience it?' Please elaborate, Pastor Bychkov."

With his eyeglasses glinting under the hot studio lights, the Baptist leaned forward and, in a dignified manner, began to explain the simple plan of salvation as contained in John 3:16.

Even as he spoke, I could hardly believe that this was happening. For here we were, making a weekly program for national television in Russia seen by 110 million viewers, and we were answering the most fundamental questions that concerned the spiritual well being of not only individual citizens, but also of the whole nation. It was, in my eyes, a major miracle.

As extraordinary as that, was the fact that we had Boris Morgunov, who until recently had each night produced the 8:00 p.m. evening news on Soviet National Television. Boris was a "double miracle man" for all of us in the ministry. As a

Jew he had accepted Christ as his Messiah and as a highly professional person in television, he had quit his job in Moscow to join our Christian television ministry.

The thirty minutes of our show was all too quickly up and I concluded the program with a challenge to the viewer to "make a personal decision" to receive Jesus Christ as God and Savior in his or her life "on the basis of what you have just heard."

I then again looked directly into the camera with all the compassion I could muster for the millions of Slavic faces that would be watching me and I closed with "the sinner's prayer."

This had special significance in Russia as many of the letters we received stated that the viewer did not know how to pray even the most elementary prayer. In fact, most had never prayed a single prayer in their lives. The prayers that we said "on air" were frequently written down by our viewers on paper and repeated untold times right across this massive land.

At the conclusion of the taping, I surveyed our state-of-the-art television equipment that was worth over $1 million U.S. The Christian Broadcasting Network and the Trinity Broadcasting Network, had contributed in a wonderful way in both funds and equipment. Once again, the magnitude of the financial miracle had me awestruck.

Just before the final credits began to roll, our Moscow counseling office address appeared on screen. The viewer had the opportunity to write in for further spiritual help and, more importantly, to receive a New Testament or a Bible.

Of course, our question and answer show was not the only program we produced. For example, when we made a three-part program series, "The Great Questions of Life," we received 60,000 response letters from Central Russia. This illustrated, to both Laura and me, the deep spiritual hunger of the Russian people after decades of devastating communism and atheism.

The emphasis of the ministry had by now shifted from radio to television. We were now on the air numerous hours a week, on the State networks of Russia, Ukraine, Belorus, Estonia, Latvia, Lithuania, Moldova, to name a few.

We produced many kinds of programs and one was particularly well received. It was a twelve-part television series on the Ten Commandments and how they related to contemporary society in the former Soviet Union. Each show included street interviews, asking people how they interpreted the commandments pertaining to that particular program. That was followed by my ten to fifteen-minute message explaining the significance of the values presented in the commandments to personal relationships and in our societies.

The series was so well liked, that the National Library of Ukraine, requested the series on video to be distributed to every library in Ukraine, the second most populous of the newly Independent States with some 54 million living there.

We now had a cumulative weekly viewing audience of 180 million people with the response of already over five million letters. The "Iron Curtain" had definitely dropped and was replaced by freedom unparalleled in the history of the vast expanse of the former USSR.

* * * * *

I was in my car on the way home on Sunday, October 3, 1993. As I cruised along the main highway between the studio and our home, I casually turned on the radio and gasped at what I heard.

"A mob of thousands of people, many armed with automatic weapons and grenades, have just set out for the Ostankino television center," the Finnish news anchor read on Radio 1, Helsinki.

I could hardly believe what I was hearing. Another coup in the making. This strategically important television center in Moscow was being attacked. Just two days before, Laura and I had stood in the lobby of the Ostankino center. We had stood beside the special Ministry of Interior commando units clad in bullet proof vests, toting automatic weapons, there to protect the complex. Although the mood already on that Friday was extremely tense, no one in the building could have believed that an attack would take place just 48 hours later. People there still hoped for a peaceful solution of the stalemate between Boris Yeltsin and some of his opponents.

As soon as I had parked the car in the driveway of our home, I hurried inside to turn on our satellite television in the living room. I quickly locked onto the satellite that was transmitting round the clock unedited footage as it happened from the White House area. Cable Network News (CNN) television cameras located on nearby rooftops were pointed towards the White House. And VTRs (video tape recorders) housed at CNN's headquarters in Atlanta, were videotaping everything that happened.

Concern for the safety of our staff in Moscow caused me to pick up the phone. I called our office in Moscow to find out about the whereabouts of our TV crew. I discovered that they were editing a program in our mobile unit (donated by Crossroads Family Of Ministries) some 10 miles from the TV center.

Boris came on the line. "Are you all right and are you aware of what is going on in Moscow?" I asked.

"What is going on?" he asked, puzzled. "We've been in the mobile unit for the past four hours."

"Boris, the TV center and the White House are under attack," I told him. "There's a fierce fire-fight going on for control of the television center."

That night, as our crew returned to their flat adjacent to Ostankino, the situation was chaotic. They had entered the apartment complex, crouching to dodge the showers of automatic weapons fire whizzing overhead.

Only later did we find out that the lone casualty of the television staff at Ostankino was our good friend, Vladimir Krasilnikov, who had regularly supplied us with difficult-to-get footage we needed for our programming. Vladimir had been editing an evening news bulletin inside the center when the armed mob opened fire on the building. The tragedy was that he had apparently been killed by "friendly fire," when crack troops, loyal to Yeltsin, had entered the building to defend it. Working out of an editing suite on the second floor, he had walked out into the hallway to see what the noise was all about. He did not know that the special troops who were not aware of his presence had orders to open fire on anything that moved in the hallways. He was cut down in a hail of bullets.

Back in our home, Laura and I sat spellbound as we witnessed every shot fired by tanks on the White House as it happened. It was bizarre. Even more unusual for us was listening to the CNN camera operators talking to each other. One of them complained that his coffee had "still not arrived" even though he had requested it twenty minutes before. "Got a cigarette?" he asked his colleague. Before his colleague could answer, there was the loud roar of cannon fire from the street below.

"Wow, did you...? What was that...? "Can you believe...? They've opened fire on the White House and we've got ringside seats."

What I did not know at that moment was that Vice-President Alexander V. Rutskoi, in full battle dress, had shouted into a radio telephone for army and air force units to come to the aid of the White House, but nobody answered the call. One of Russia's best-known reporters, Vyachislav Terekhov, was on the scene, and Rutskoi enlisted him as a mediator. The vice-president told him the numerous conditions for the surrender of the hard-line deputies rebelling against the government of President Yeltsin. The reporter relayed the terms through his office to Prime Minister Viktor S. Chernomyrdin, and a few minutes later he received by phone the response. "The surrender," he was told, "must be unconditional."

When he told the news to Rutskoi, the vice-president of Russia capitulated immediately, and the reporter was given a white linen and told to head outside to continue the talks. But on his way out, one of the numerous paramilitary bands defending the parliament, grabbed him, beat him and threw him in the basement, where he remained until mid-afternoon.

Suddenly, tank fire tore holes into a floor of the Parliament building, sending up white smoke as thousands of pieces of paper were blown out of the building and down into the street below. I winced with shock as suddenly another 125-millimeter shell from a Russian tank slammed into the white-marbled building. The whole structure shook with its impact and the picture began to momentarily shake as the scene was being relayed around the world.

I was overwhelmed with anxiety, fear and shock as I watched the drama unfold some 1,000 miles away.

I prayed, "Oh God, whatever happens, please allow the Gospel to continue to sound over national radio and television. There are millions who still need to hear of Your love for them and that there is forgiveness and reconciliation in the blood of Jesus."

Back at the White House, the negotiations faltered, and the siege of the mortally wounded Russian Parliament building continued for hours more.

When it all ended after two bloody days, nearly 200 people lay dead. It was the worst spasm of political violence that Moscow had seen since the Bolshevik Revolution more than 70 years previously. It had been an event marked by fear, anger and chaos.

People stumbled out of the area that was soon to be known as the "Black House" waving white flags. They had been convinced that the "masses of Moscow" would rise up with them and sweep away Yeltsin's government, but now they felt the bitter taste of defeat in their mouths.

Shortly afterwards, I traveled to Moscow and joined hundreds of ordinary Muscovites, staring glassy-eyed at the charred shell of the White House, the skyscraper parliament sardonically renamed "The Black House." I reflected how that, three years into the country's heart-wrenching drift to reinvent itself, it all could have been brought to a screeching halt had the coup been successful.

The coup plotters had tried to turn back the clock of history, but it was now moving in another direction and the USSR was splintered into many different pieces.

But thank God it was "time out," and we were still able to freely present the Gospel on national television across Russia and many of the other independent states of the CIS.

At least, for the moment, we could continue our work with International Russian Radio\TV.

Mobile unit donated by Crossroads Family of Ministries of
Toronto, Ontario, Canada.

Chapter Thirty

No Faith—No Democracy

So, what of the future in the former Soviet Union? Well, it all looks very precarious at this time. For instance, Russian right-winger Vladimir Zhirinovsky told me he would stop all western religious organizations from operating in Russia if he were elected leader of Russia.

I learned of this during a television interview with the 47-year-old ultra-nationalist in March of 1994, during a brief visit he made to Helsinki. What he told me will send chills down the spines of Western Christians working in the Russian Republic.

"We will stop all western Christians, Eastern religions [and] the Muslims," he said. "We don't need religious cosmopolitanism. We will, in every way, limit all religious activity that is foreign to us."

Zhirinovsky also said that the political leadership of the country, under his leadership and that of the Orthodox patri-

242

arch of Moscow, would decide which groups would have the right to religious activity. But, he added, the present patriarch needed to be replaced. "He is weak," said the leader of the Liberal Democrat Party of Russia. I thought it was odd that he would attack Metropolitan Alexei. After all, he was the highest authority in the Russian Orthodox Church.

In a rambling conversation, the man whose party stunned the world in December of 1994 by winning almost a quarter of the party vote in Russia's parliamentary elections, garnering more than 60 seats in the 450-seat lower house or Duma, outlined that the Russia he wanted would be a land of Orthodoxy, free from Western religious influences. He recently showed his devotion to the Russian Orthodox Church when he was baptized. But very obviously, Zhirinovsky had no in-depth knowledge of religion. He also voiced his distaste for Jews. This would be understandable if his father had been a Jew, as has been reported. He would want to cover that up in a country where there is so much anti-Semitism.

When I asked him if he had any religious convictions, he replied, "Yes, of course. From childhood I...where I was born, in the city of Vernyi, towards India and China...here was a church. Grandmother was a believer. I have her Bible, the one she forced me to read...I have it at home.

"In school and at college, there was naturally no religious education. I took two courses in scientific atheism. That, of course, disrupted the development of faith in me. But, inside, I always held onto [my] convictions. I, myself, am an Orthodox, baptized. I think more than anything, Orthodox Christianity...Orthodoxy... is inside Christianity."

When I challenged his views against Western religious groups, saying that the Bible advocates tolerance, he responded, "Tolerance...yes, tolerance. Let everyone proclaim its own, so to speak, but let them not interfere with each other. Tolerate and don't interfere in the affairs of other countries. We are not pushing our lifestyles on anyone else."

RING THOSE ORTHODOX BELLS

Vladimir Zhirinovsky was then asked to describe the role of the church in a nation ruled by himself. "In my book, *The*

Surge Southward, I wrote that I wanted the ring of the bells of the Russian Orthodox Church to be heard from the northern sea to the Indian Ocean. The ring is needed for the tranquillity of the soul and for the reinforcement of the nation."

These were spooky words as they actually mean that the church would be used as a tool to achieve Mr. Zhirinovsky's political goals.

When I challenged him as saying something that sounded "threatening to the Protestant churches of Russia," Zhirinovsky responded, "To whom? No, I am not against Christian [churches]. I mean mainly Eastern religions and the Muslims. Let's say Baptists, Adventists, Lutherans [and] Pentecostals...Let them coexist. The only thing I am against is pressuring the Orthodox Church and their priests."

I then asked the controversial Russian if his baptism in the Orthodox Church was anything but a political maneuver.

"It was not a political maneuver," he declared. "It has to do with the history of our people and the fact that the church for one thousand years has played a spiritual role in the consciousness of our nation."

I then told Zhirinovsky that Western Christians "have brought millions of Bibles into Russia." The political leader then revealed that he owns "about twenty Bibles." He went on to say, "The most precious one is from my grandmother. From it, I have read the very first lines [of Scripture.] She asked me to read it to her as her eyes were already bad. I was thirteen then."

When asked his favorite book or passage in the Bible, he was at a total loss on how to answer. Finally, he said, that he most of all enjoyed reading about "the places that are dedicated to the soul." Zhirinovsky added, "The historic passages, where all that wandering in the wilderness [is recorded]. It is history [and] it has meaning."

If it was true that Zhirinovsky's father was a Jew, then this would explain his recollection of the event from his childhood home as the story of the Exodus was recounted in Jewish families.

When I asked what he thought about Jesus Christ, he responded, "Well, it is the image of man—God, the ideal for men, that people strive for because He dedicated Himself to serving God." I was mildly surprised at this remark. Although it reflected more depth, it also unveiled his interest in Jesus's popularity, rather than who He really was.

I then raised the thorny questions of the Russian Jews and said that Zhirinovsky had been quoted as being against Jews.

"They [the Jews] are misbehaving in Russia," he claimed. "They are trying to destroy Russia. They are aggressive, cruel, and hate everything that is Russian." At this point, Zhirinovsky abruptly cut himself off and changed the subject.

"By the way, my grandmother was a Baptist. Her name is in the church registry in the Baptist Church in Alma Ata. She would bring me to church. So I am all for Christian confessions (denominations)."

I then stated that America was "a Christian nation." I wanted to know what kind of relations he would seek with the United States of America.

Vladimir Zhirinovsky said he wanted normal relations that were peaceful and equal. "But," he went on to say, "we are against America pretending to lord it over all, in areas that have traditionally been ours: Eastern Europe, the south... the southern nations bordering Russia: Afghanistan, Iran, Turkey, China and Japan.

"We don't lay claim to Asia, China, India and Japan. We are concerned about our neighbors: Finland, Poland, Slovakia, Hungary, Romania, Turkey, Iran, Afghanistan, China and Japan."

Interestingly, both lists contained China and Japan and this was typical of his contradictory style. I then said that "some people consider you possessed." The Russian leader said, "Well, in principle you need to be in order to lift up those [who have] gone astray, that no longer believe. Those dogged by the latest political doctrines. There is a kind of need to be possessed, otherwise there is no way to pull the people out of the ideological abyss they are in."

I concluded by asking Zhirinovsky if he felt he was led by God.

"Yes, yes, yes," he replied.

This interview was clearly not what I had expected, because during it, Zhirinovsky wound down from his normal aggressive, interruptive, vocal style. I can only believe the Holy Spirit calmed him down. It was as if he enjoyed talking about his personal views on religion.

THE BRAWL

After concluding the interview, Vladimir Zhirinovsky headed back to Moscow where he sparked outraged protests when he physically assaulted an ex-colleague who had announced he was quitting the ultra-nationalist's parliamentary faction.

Witnesses said that a conversation between Zhirinovsky and defector Vladimir Borzyuk quickly degenerated into a vicious brawl, with the pro-fascist leader grabbing the former comrade and banging his head against the wall.

Liberal lawmaker Valerie Borschov, who was walking past at the time, jumped to Borzyuk's defense, but was himself assaulted by the impassioned Zhirinovsky who said he would "see him rot in prison."

The leader of the misnamed Liberal Democrat Party next attacked a Russian journalist who had taped the incident, demanding he destroy the cassette, then seizing the tape recorder and smashing it when he refused.

The incident happened after the Duma rejected an attempt by Zhirinovsky to push through the so-called "imperative mandate," a procedure that would entail the dismissal of any deputy who failed to observe party discipline—a move that may have affected further defections from his party.

I wonder why I am not surprised by Vladimir Zhirinovsky's outrageous behavior.

After all, this is the same man who threatened Germany and Japan with nuclear war, and pledged to revive the Soviet Union and expand Russia's borders into Eastern Europe.

* * * * *

There are fifty ways of saying "to steal" in Russian, according to Claire Sterling, author of the book, *Crime Without Frontiers*. She states, "...the Russian Mafia uses them all. It is the world's largest, busiest and possibly meanest collection of organized hoods, consisting of 5,000 gangs and three million people who work for or with them.

The writer states that the Soviet Mafia's reach extends into all fifteen of the former Soviet republics, across eleven time zones and one-sixth of the earth's land mass.

"It intrudes into every field of Western concern; the nascent free market, privatization, disarmament, foreign humanitarian relief and financial aid, even state reserves of currency and gold.

"Here was the church's grand opportunity to contribute in a very meaningful way. If any nation ever needed Biblical values, that nation is Russia. Sadly, as communism failed, another terrible yoke has descended like a black cloud over the land. The Russian Mafia is a league of racketeers without equal.

"Unlike the Mafia in Sicily, which is admired and copied, it has no home seat or central command," says Sterling. "There are no ancestral memories or common bloodlines. But its proliferating clans are invading every sphere of Russian life, usurping political power, taking over state enterprises and fleecing natural resources.

"They are engaged in extortion, theft, forgery, armed assault, contract killing, swindling, drug running, arms smuggling, prostitution, gambling, loan sharking, embezzling, money laundering and black-marketing—all on a monumental and increasingly international scale."

This scourge on the Russian people has risen from the ruins of the Soviet empire. Korruptsiya (corruption) is spreading uncontrollably as the whole fabric of society falls apart and becomes the curse of a stricken nation.

"Corruption," Boris Yeltsin said in 1992, "is devouring the State from top to bottom."

It is a malignant growth that could one day strangle and destroy all of Soviet life. Unless we pray!

* * * * *

OPEN PERSECUTION COMING

Svetlana Nevrova was stabbed sixty times and left for dead in a ditch in Ukraine. This nineteen-year-old evangelical who loved to sing in her church choir, was laid to rest on January 15, 1994.

Larissa Detyura, a twenty-year-old Baptist woman, was murdered on January 7 in Maykop, Russia. She had been kidnapped and murdered, then brought home and tossed into her yard. Afterwards, anonymous death threats appeared in her parents' mailbox.

These stories and others were brought to Capitol Hill in Washington, D.C., in late March by a Russian evangelical leader as evidence that the window of religious freedom in the former Soviet Union is already slamming shut.

Boris Perchatkin, came to America to try to alert the West that the republics of the region were fast becoming strongholds of religious persecution—this time against Protestants.

The West first learned of this through a bill introduced in the former Russian legislature that would have restricted non-Orthodox activity. The bill failed when Boris Yeltsin dismissed Parliament in 1993.

"One-and-a half years ago I myself didn't believe this was going on," said Perchatkin, as reported in Baptist Press. "But as I am working more and more on it, this horrible picture is forming. We have a very short time."

Who would be better able to recognize the bloody slashes on religious freedom, than a dissident believer?

In Washington, D.C., he met with U.S. congressmen, State Department officials, and advisers to President Clinton. He told them the former Soviet Union—widely viewed as relatively free despite its growing pains — is actually a time bomb of persecution that, when it explodes, will vent unimaginable horror.

Perchatkin warned that after the next Russian presidential elections in 1996—if not earlier—wide-spread, open persecution of Protestants will become the rule in Russia. He predicts a systematic "cleansing" of Protestants, similar to that experienced by all faiths under Joseph Stalin, as nationalists tout the Orthodox and Muslim religions as "ours."

This man's grandfather was a Baptist pastor when Stalin came to power. "Over the course of five years, his community was physically destroyed," Perchatkin said. "Between 1928 and 1933 nine people were shot, including my grandfather. Three people survived. The rest were sent to prisons and labor camps, or just disappeared."

"But extremist Muslims are only part of the danger. An alarming alliance was forged in February 1994 when the Russian army opened its arms to a military organization which is about one million strong, with historical roots in the Cossack people. It has declared its allegiance to Russian Orthodoxy—and war against Protestants," wrote Marty Croll.

All of this shows us two things:

1. The window of opportunity in the former Soviet Union may be extremely slim. That is why it is vital for us to seize the opportunity now.

2. The cleansing out of communism has not been replaced by something good. In Matthew 12:44, we read that Jesus said, "When an evil spirit comes out of a man, it goes through arid places seeking rest and does not find it. Then it says, 'I will return to the house I left.' When it arrives, it finds the house unoccupied, swept clean and put it in order. Then it goes and takes with it seven other spirits more wicked than itself, and go in and live there. And the final condition of that man is worse than the first."

Isn't this what has happened in the former Soviet Union? One demon has been driven out, but what has it been replaced with? The Russian Mafia, corruption on a massive scale, violence, hunger and hatred.

Before the "seven other spirits more wicked than itself" completely take over the former Soviet Union, we need to fill that nation with the Good News of Jesus Christ. Otherwise I dread to think about what lies ahead.

Hannu interviewing Vladimir Zhirinovsky in Helsinki.

Epilogue

Nikita Khruschev, Soviet Communist Party Chief in the 1950s and 1960s declared to his nation, "By 1980, we will put the last Christian on display on national television." A rather bold statement. Today, Mr. Khruschev lies in his grave but the Church in Russia lives on — stronger than ever.

In the last eight years of openness and reform in the world's once greatest atheistic society, the Gospel has been proclaimed in a way that has no precedent, yet the job is not done.

The work has barely begun. After 70 years of desolation and godlessness, the nation struggles to find values of which it was stripped generations earlier. Russia is seeking a long-lost faith in the God who wasn't supposed to exist.

There is not a prophet who is able to accurately tell what lies ahead for Russia and her millions — for whom Christ Jesus died.

We do know that there is much work ahead. For the moment, IRR/TV continues to telecast on over 30 regional television channels. A special follow-up magazine goes out to hundreds of thousands of families across Russia — to those who have responded to the proclaimed message on radio and television.

Shortly before this book went to press, Russia State Television has, rather unexpectedly, offered IRR/TV one hour of television time daily to an audience of 70 million. In the present political climate this is a miracle. It is critical to seize the op-

251

portunity and use it — though we have few resources for the job. But miracles of God have never been dependent on great resources. They have however, always required one resource — faith. So, as the title of this book declares, God asks us to "ONLY BELIEVE."

Yes, no matter what the circumstances, God asks us to be obedient. Every day of our ministry to Russia has required one thing — that we only believe. With that attitude, God can do anything in each of our lives, and in any ministry. May the Lord bless you as you exercise faith in Him with whom all things are possible.

Hannu Haukka